JUST **1** POT

JUST **1** POT

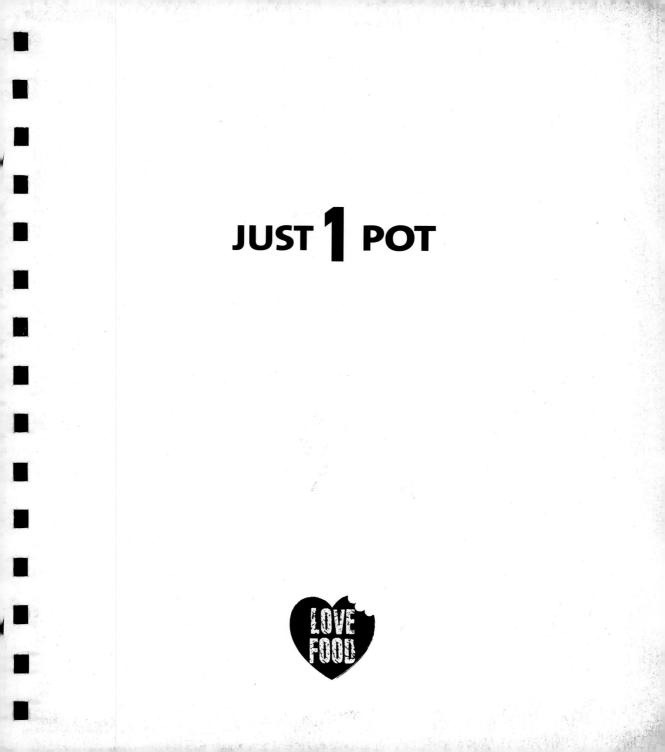

LOVE
FOOD

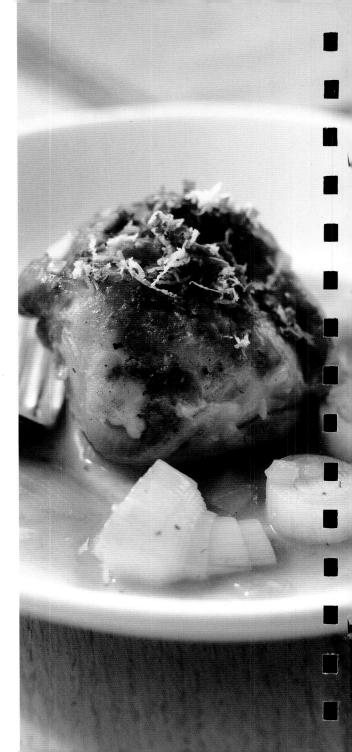

Love Food ® is an imprint of
Parragon Books Ltd

Parragon
Queen Street House
4 Queen Street
Bath BA1 1HE, UK

Love Food ® and the accompanying heart
device is a trademark of Parragon Books Ltd

Design: Terry Jeavons & Company

ISBN 978-1-4075-3389-6

Printed in China

This book uses imperial, metric, and US cup
measurements. Follow the same units of
measurement throughout; do not mix imperial
and metric. All spoon measurements are
level, unless otherwise stated: teaspoons are
assumed to be 5ml, and tablespoons are
assumed to be 15ml. Unless otherwise stated,
milk is assumed to be whole-fat, eggs and
individual fruits, such as bananas, are medium,
and pepper is freshly ground black pepper.

Recipes using raw or very lightly cooked eggs
should be avoided by children, the elderly,
pregnant women, convalescents, and anyone
with an illness. Pregnant and breast-feeding
women are advised to avoid eating peanuts
and peanut products.

Contents

Introduction

If you love to cook but can't face washing the dishes, then *Just 1 Pot* is the book for you. As the name suggests, all the dishes can be cooked in a single pot, leaving you with very little to clean up, and plenty of time to relax while the cooking takes care of itself.

As well as cutting down on the cleaning up, one-pot cooking has so many other benefits.

- It's ideal for people with limited cooking space or equipment. If you're a college student, or planning a camping vacation, or simply spending some time in temporary accommodation, you will find it invaluable.

- It's a healthy way of cooking. You don't need a lot of fat and all the vitamins and minerals go into the cooking juices.

- You'll be saving energy by cooking on a single burner.

- Most recipes are flexible and can be adjusted to the ingredients you have on hand.

- It's the ideal food for potluck suppers and feeding a crowd. One large pot is convenient to transport and the food can be served directly from it.

One-pot cooking doesn't limit you to soups and stews, although there are plenty of recipes for these in the book. In many parts of the world, cooking in a single pot is the norm, whether it's in a baking dish or roasting pan, a skillet or wok, a tagine or a Dutch oven. The wide choice of pots and pans opens up endless possibilities, allowing you to add all kinds of dishes and techniques to your one-pot repertoire. Spicy stir-fries and curries, fragrant rice and pasta dishes, gratins, bakes, and braises are all easy to make in just one pan or pot.

You'll find chapters on meat and poultry, both of which develop marvelous flavors and succulent textures when cooked in a single pot. The chapter on fish and seafood includes classic soups and stews, as well as fish and rice combinations that can be cooked in a wide pan on the stovetop. Vegetables

develop rich aromas and delectable textures from one-pot cooking, too. The treatment works equally well for desserts. Pies, crumbles, and puddings can all be baked in a single dish and brought straight from the stove to the table.

As the recipes show, this no-frills way of cooking is wonderfully time-saving and, because everything is ready at the same time, the ultimate in convenience. Just put the pot on the table and tuck in.

1 Meat

Long, slow cooking in an enclosed pot is the ideal method for bringing out the best in cuts of meat that are too tough for frying or roasting. Enjoy the rich mellow flavors of post-roast pork, or fruity Mediterranean lamb with apricots. Spice lovers will enjoy palate-tingling chili con carne or a Caribbean-style pepper-pot stew. The moist heat encourages a magical exchange of flavors between meat, vegetables, and seasonings, resulting in truly succulent and meltingly tender dishes.

Pot Roast with Potatoes & Dill

INGREDIENTS

serves 6

2½ tbsp all-purpose flour

1 tsp salt

¼ tsp pepper

1 rolled brisket joint,
weighing 3 lb 8 oz/1.6 kg

2 tbsp vegetable oil

2 tbsp butter

1 onion, finely chopped

2 celery stalks, diced

2 carrots, peeled and diced

1 tsp dill seed

1 tsp dried thyme or oregano

1½ cups red wine

⅔–1 cup beef stock

4–5 potatoes, cut into large
chunks and boiled until just
tender

2 tbsp chopped fresh dill,
to serve

1 Preheat the oven to 275°F/140°C. Mix 2 tablespoons of the flour with the salt and pepper in a shallow dish. Dip the meat to coat. Heat the oil in a flameproof casserole and brown the meat all over. Transfer to a plate.

2 Add half the butter to the casserole and cook the onion, celery, carrots, dill seed, and thyme for 5 minutes. Return the meat and juices to the casserole.

3 Pour in the wine and enough stock to reach one-third of the way up the meat. Bring to a boil, cover, and cook in the oven for 3 hours, turning the meat every 30 minutes. After it has been cooking for 2 hours, add the potatoes and more stock if necessary.

4 When ready, transfer the meat and vegetables to a warmed serving dish. Strain the cooking liquid to remove any solids, then return the liquid to the casserole.

5 Mix the remaining butter and flour to a paste. Bring the cooking liquid to a boil. Whisk in small pieces of the flour and butter paste, whisking constantly until the sauce is smooth. Pour the sauce over the meat and vegetables. Sprinkle with the fresh dill to serve.

Beef in Beer with Herb Dumplings

INGREDIENTS

serves 6

2 tbsp corn oil

2 large onions, thinly sliced

8 carrots, sliced

4 tbsp all-purpose flour

2 lb 12 oz/1.25 kg braising
beef, cut into cubes

generous 1¾ cups stout

2 tsp brown sugar

2 bay leaves

1 tbsp chopped fresh thyme

salt and pepper

HERB DUMPLINGS

heaping ¾ cup self-rising
flour

pinch of salt

½ cup lard

2 tbsp chopped fresh parsley,
plus extra to garnish

about 4 tbsp water

1 Preheat the oven to 325°F/160°C. Heat the oil in a flameproof casserole. Add the onions and carrots and cook over low heat, stirring occasionally, for 5 minutes, or until the onions are softened. Meanwhile, place the flour in a plastic bag and season with salt and pepper. Add the braising beef to the bag, tie the top, and shake well to coat. Do this in batches, if necessary.

2 Remove the vegetables from the casserole with a slotted spoon and reserve. Add the braising beef to the casserole, in batches, and cook, stirring frequently, until browned all over. Return all the meat and the onions and carrots to the casserole and sprinkle in any remaining seasoned flour. Pour in the stout and add the sugar, bay leaves, and thyme. Bring to a boil, cover, and transfer to the preheated oven to bake for 1¾ hours.

3 To make the herb dumplings, sift the flour and salt into a bowl. Stir in the lard and parsley and add enough of the water to make a soft dough. Shape into small balls between the palms of your hands. Add to the casserole and return to the oven for 30 minutes. Remove and discard the bay leaves and serve, sprinkled with parsley.

Daube of Beef

INGREDIENTS

serves 6

1½ cups dry white wine

2 tbsp brandy

1 tbsp white wine vinegar

4 shallots, sliced

4 carrots, sliced

1 garlic clove, finely chopped

6 black peppercorns

4 fresh thyme sprigs

1 fresh rosemary sprig

2 fresh parsley sprigs, plus
extra to garnish

1 bay leaf

1 lb 10 oz/750 g beef top round,
cut into 1-inch/2.5-cm cubes

2 tbsp olive oil

1 lb 12 oz/800 g canned
chopped tomatoes

8 oz/225 g portobello
mushrooms, sliced

strip of finely pared orange
rind

2 oz/55 g prosciutto, cut into
strips

12 black olives

salt

1 Combine the wine, brandy, vinegar, shallots, carrots, garlic, peppercorns, thyme, rosemary, parsley, and bay leaf and season to taste with salt. Add the beef, stirring to coat, then cover with plastic wrap and let marinate in the refrigerator for 8 hours, or overnight.

2 Preheat the oven to 300°F/150°C. Drain the beef, reserving the marinade, and pat dry on paper towels. Heat half the oil in a large, flameproof casserole. Add the beef cubes in batches and cook over medium heat, stirring, for 3–4 minutes, or until browned. Transfer the beef to a plate with a slotted spoon. Brown the remaining beef, adding more oil, if necessary.

3 Return all of the beef to the casserole and add the tomatoes and their juices, mushrooms, and orange rind. Strain the reserved marinade into the casserole. Bring to a boil, cover, and cook in the oven for 2½ hours.

4 Remove the casserole from the oven, add the prosciutto and olives, and return it to the oven to cook for an additional 30 minutes, or until the beef is very tender. Discard the orange rind and serve straight from the casserole, garnished with parsley.

Beef Goulash

INGREDIENTS

serves 4

2 tbsp vegetable oil

1 large onion, chopped

1 garlic clove, crushed

1 lb 10 oz/750 g lean braising beef

2 tbsp paprika

15 oz/425 g can chopped tomatoes

2 tbsp tomato paste

1 large red bell pepper, seeded and chopped

6 oz/175 g button mushrooms, sliced

2½ cups beef stock

1 tbsp cornstarch

1 tbsp water

4 tbsp lowfat plain yogurt

paprika, for sprinkling

salt and pepper

chopped fresh parsley, to garnish

freshly cooked long-grain and wild rice, to serve

1 Heat the vegetable oil in a large pan and cook the onion and garlic for 3–4 minutes.

2 Cut the braising beef into chunks and cook over a high heat for 3 minutes, until browned all over. Add the paprika and stir well, then add the chopped tomatoes, tomato paste, bell pepper, and mushrooms. Cook for 2 minutes, stirring frequently.

3 Pour in the beef stock. Bring to a boil, then reduce the heat. Cover and simmer for 1½–2 hours, until the meat is tender.

4 Blend the cornstarch with the water, then add to the pan, stirring until thickened and smooth. Cook for 1 minute, then season with salt and pepper to taste.

5 Put the yogurt in a serving bowl and sprinkle with a little paprika.

6 Transfer the beef goulash to a warmed serving dish, garnish with chopped fresh parsley, and serve with rice and yogurt.

Chili con Carne

INGREDIENTS

serves ❹

1 lb 10 oz/750 g lean braising beef

2 tbsp vegetable oil

1 large onion, sliced

2–4 garlic cloves, crushed

1 tbsp all-purpose flour

generous 1¾ cups tomato juice

14 oz/400 g canned tomatoes

1–2 tbsp sweet chili sauce

1 tsp ground cumin

15 oz/425 g canned red kidney beans, drained and rinsed

½ tsp dried oregano

1–2 tbsp chopped fresh parsley

salt and pepper

sprigs of fresh herbs, to garnish

freshly cooked rice, to serve

tortillas, to serve

1 Preheat the oven to 325°F/160°C. Using a sharp knife, cut the beef into ¾-inch/2-cm cubes. Heat the vegetable oil in a large flameproof casserole and cook the beef over medium heat until well sealed on all sides. Remove the beef from the casserole with a slotted spoon and set aside until required.

2 Add the onion and garlic to the casserole and cook until lightly browned; then stir in the flour and cook for 1–2 minutes.

3 Stir in the tomato juice and tomatoes and bring to a boil. Return the beef to the casserole and add the chili sauce, cumin, and salt and pepper to taste. Cover and cook in the preheated oven for 1½ hours, or until the beef is almost tender.

4 Stir in the kidney beans, oregano, and parsley, and adjust the seasoning to taste, if necessary. Cover the casserole and return to the oven for 45 minutes. Transfer to 4 large, warmed serving plates, garnish with sprigs of fresh herbs, and serve immediately with freshly cooked rice and tortillas.

Beef & Vegetable Stew with Corn

INGREDIENTS

serves ❹

1 lb/450 g braising beef

1½ tbsp all-purpose flour

1 tsp hot paprika

1–1½ tsp chili powder

1 tsp ground ginger

2 tbsp olive oil

1 large onion, cut into chunks

3 garlic cloves, sliced

2 celery stalks, sliced

8 oz/225 g carrots, chopped

1¼ cups lager

1¼ cups beef stock

12 oz/350 g potatoes, chopped

1 red bell pepper, seeded and chopped

2 corn cobs, halved

4 oz/115 g tomatoes, cut into quarters

1 cup shelled fresh or frozen peas

1 tbsp chopped fresh cilantro

salt and pepper

1 Trim any fat or gristle from the beef and cut into 1-inch/2.5-cm chunks. Mix the flour and spices together. Toss the beef in the spiced flour until well coated.

2 Heat the oil in a large, heavy-bottom pan and cook the onion, garlic, and celery, stirring frequently, for 5 minutes, or until softened. Add the beef and cook over high heat, stirring frequently, for 3 minutes, or until browned on all sides and sealed.

3 Add the carrots, then remove from the heat. Gradually stir in the lager and stock, then return to the heat and bring to a boil, stirring. Reduce the heat, then cover and simmer, stirring occasionally, for 1½ hours.

4 Add the potatoes to the pan and simmer for an additional 15 minutes. Add the red bell pepper and corn cobs and simmer for 15 minutes, then add the tomatoes and peas and simmer for an additional 10 minutes, or until the beef and vegetables are tender. Season to taste with salt and pepper, then stir in the cilantro and serve.

Beef Stroganoff

INGREDIENTS

serves **4**

½ oz/15 g dried porcini
mushrooms

12 oz/350 g beef tenderloin

2 tbsp olive oil

4 oz/115 g shallots, sliced

6 oz/175 g cremini
mushrooms

½ tsp **Dijon mustard**

5 tbsp heavy cream

salt and pepper

freshly cooked pasta,
to serve

fresh chives, to garnish

1 Place the dried porcini mushrooms in a bowl
and cover with hot water. Let soak for 20 minutes.
Meanwhile, cut the beef against the grain into
¼-inch/5-mm thick slices, then into ½-inch/1-cm
long strips, and reserve.

2 Drain the mushrooms, reserving the soaking
liquid, and chop. Strain the soaking liquid
through a fine-mesh strainer or coffee filter
and reserve.

3 Heat half the oil in a large skillet. Add the
shallots and cook over low heat, stirring
occasionally, for 5 minutes, or until softened.
Add the dried mushrooms, reserved soaking
water, and whole cremini mushrooms and cook,
stirring frequently, for 10 minutes, or until
almost all of the liquid has evaporated, then
transfer the mixture to a plate.

4 Heat the remaining oil in the skillet, add the
beef, and cook, stirring frequently, for 4 minutes,
or until browned all over. You may need to do
this in batches. Return the mushroom mixture
to the skillet and season to taste with salt and
pepper. Place the mustard and cream in a small
bowl and stir to mix, then fold into the mixture.
Heat through gently, then serve with freshly
cooked pasta, garnished with chives.

Pepper Pot-Style Stew

INGREDIENTS

serves **4**

1 lb/450 g braising beef

1½ tbsp all-purpose flour

2 tbsp olive oil

1 red onion, chopped

3–4 garlic cloves, crushed

1 fresh green chile, seeded and chopped

3 celery stalks, sliced

4 whole cloves

1 tsp ground allspice

1–2 tsp hot pepper sauce, or to taste

2½ cups beef stock

8 oz/225 g seeded and peeled squash, such as acorn, cut into small chunks

1 large red bell pepper, seeded and chopped

4 tomatoes, coarsely chopped

4 oz/115 g okra, trimmed and halved

mixed wild and basmati rice, to serve

1 Trim any fat or gristle from the beef and cut into 1-inch/2.5-cm chunks. Toss the beef in the flour until well coated and reserve any remaining flour.

2 Heat the oil in a large, heavy-bottom pan and cook the onion, garlic, chile, and celery with the cloves and allspice, stirring frequently, for 5 minutes, or until softened. Add the beef and cook over high heat, stirring frequently, for 3 minutes, or until browned on all sides and sealed. Sprinkle in the reserved flour and cook, stirring constantly, for 2 minutes, then remove from the heat.

3 Add the hot pepper sauce and gradually stir in the stock, then return to the heat and bring to a boil, stirring. Reduce the heat, then cover and simmer, stirring occasionally, for 1½ hours.

4 Add the squash and red bell pepper to the pan and simmer for an additional 15 minutes. Add the tomatoes and okra and simmer for an additional 15 minutes, or until the beef is tender. Serve with mixed wild and basmati rice.

Osso Bucco

INGREDIENTS

serves 4

1 tbsp virgin olive oil

4 tbsp butter

2 onions, chopped

1 leek, sliced

3 tbsp all-purpose flour

4 thick slices of veal shin (osso bucco)

1¼ cups white wine

1¼ cups veal or chicken stock

salt and pepper

GREMOLATA

2 tbsp chopped fresh parsley

1 garlic clove, chopped finely

grated rind of 1 lemon

1 Heat the oil and butter in a large, heavy-bottom skillet. Add the onions and leek and cook over low heat, stirring occasionally, for 5 minutes, until softened.

2 Spread out the flour on a plate and season with salt and pepper. Toss the pieces of veal in the flour to coat, shaking off any excess. Add the veal to the skillet, increase the heat to high, and cook until browned on both sides.

3 Gradually stir in the wine and stock and bring just to a boil, stirring constantly. Reduce the heat, cover, and let simmer for 1¼ hours, or until the veal is very tender.

4 Meanwhile, make the gremolata by mixing the parsley, garlic, and lemon rind in a small bowl.

5 Transfer the veal to a warmed serving dish with a slotted spoon. Bring the sauce to a boil and cook, stirring occasionally, until thickened and reduced. Pour the sauce over the veal, sprinkle with the gremolata, and serve immediately.

Irish Stew

INGREDIENTS

4 tbsp all-purpose flour

3 lb/1.3 kg middle neck of lamb, trimmed of visible fat

3 large onions, chopped

3 carrots, sliced

1 lb/450 g potatoes, cut into quarters

½ tsp dried thyme

scant 3½ cups hot beef stock

2 tbsp chopped fresh parsley, to garnish

salt and pepper

serves ❹

1 Preheat the oven to 325°F/160°C. Spread the flour on a plate and season with salt and pepper. Roll the pieces of lamb in the flour to coat, shaking off any excess, and arrange in the bottom of a casserole.

2 Layer the onions, carrots, and potatoes on top of the lamb.

3 Sprinkle in the thyme and pour in the stock, then cover and cook in the preheated oven for 2½ hours. Garnish with the chopped parsley and serve straight from the casserole.

Lamb Stew with Chickpeas

INGREDIENTS

serves **4** to **6**

6 tbsp olive oil

8 oz/225 g chorizo sausage, cut into ¼-inch/5-mm thick slices, casings removed

2 large onions, chopped

6 large garlic cloves, crushed

2 lb/900 g boned leg of lamb, cut into 2-inch/5-cm chunks

scant 1¼ cups lamb stock or water

½ cup red wine, such as Rioja or Tempranillo

2 tbsp sherry vinegar

1 lb 12 oz/800 g canned chopped tomatoes

4 sprigs fresh thyme

2 bay leaves

½ tsp sweet Spanish paprika

1 lb 12 oz/800 g canned chickpeas, rinsed and drained

salt and pepper

1 Preheat the oven to 325°F/160°C. Heat 4 tablespoons of the oil in a large, heavy-bottom flameproof casserole over medium-high heat. Reduce the heat, add the chorizo, and cook for 1 minute; set aside. Add the onions to the casserole and cook for 2 minutes, then add the garlic and continue cooking for 3 minutes, or until the onions are softened, but not browned. Remove from the casserole and set aside.

2 Heat the remaining 2 tablespoons of oil in the casserole. Add the lamb cubes in a single layer without overcrowding the casserole, and cook until browned on each side; work in batches, if necessary.

3 Return the onion mixture to the casserole with all the lamb. Stir in the stock, wine, vinegar, tomatoes with their juices, and salt and pepper to taste. Bring to a boil, scraping any glazed bits from the bottom of the casserole. Reduce the heat and stir in the thyme, bay leaves, and paprika.

4 Transfer to the oven and cook, covered, for 40–45 minutes, until the lamb is tender. Stir in the chickpeas and return to the oven, uncovered, for 10 minutes, or until they are heated through and the juices are reduced.

5 Taste and adjust the seasoning. Garnish with thyme and serve.

Mediterranean Lamb with Apricots & Pistachios

INGREDIENTS

serves **4**

pinch of saffron threads

2 tbsp almost boiling water

1 lb/450 g lean boneless lamb, such as leg steaks

1½ tbsp all-purpose flour

1 tsp ground coriander

½ tsp ground cumin

½ tsp ground allspice

1 tbsp olive oil

1 onion, chopped

2–3 garlic cloves, chopped

scant 2 cups lamb or chicken stock

1 cinnamon stick, bruised

½ cup dried apricots, coarsely chopped

6 oz/175 g zucchini, sliced into semicircles

4 oz/115 g cherry tomatoes

1 tbsp chopped fresh cilantro

salt and pepper

2 tbsp coarsely chopped pistachios, to garnish

couscous, to serve

1 Put the saffron threads in a heatproof pitcher with the water and let stand for at least 10 minutes to steep. Trim off any fat or gristle from the lamb and cut into 1-inch/2.5-cm chunks. Mix the flour and spices together, then toss the lamb in the spiced flour until well coated and reserve any remaining spiced flour.

2 Heat the oil in a large, heavy-bottom pan and cook the onion and garlic, stirring frequently, for 5 minutes, or until softened. Add the lamb and cook over high heat, stirring frequently, for 3 minutes, or until browned on all sides and sealed. Sprinkle in the reserved spiced flour and cook, stirring constantly, for 2 minutes, then remove from the heat.

3 Gradually stir in the stock and the saffron and its soaking liquid, then return to the heat and bring to a boil, stirring. Add the cinnamon stick and apricots. Reduce the heat, then cover and simmer, stirring occasionally, for 1 hour.

4 Add the zucchini and tomatoes and cook for an additional 15 minutes. Discard the cinnamon stick. Stir in the fresh cilantro and season to taste with salt and pepper. Serve sprinkled with the pistachios, accompanied by couscous.

Lamb with Pears

INGREDIENTS

1 tbsp olive oil

2 lb 4 oz/1 kg best end-of-neck lamb cutlets, trimmed of visible fat

6 pears, peeled, cored, and cut into quarters

1 tsp ground ginger

4 potatoes, diced

4 tbsp hard cider

1 lb/450 g green beans

salt and pepper

2 tbsp snipped fresh chives, to garnish

serves 4

1 Preheat the oven to 325°F/160°C. Heat the olive oil in a flameproof casserole over medium heat. Add the lamb and cook, turning frequently, for 5–10 minutes, or until browned on all sides.

2 Arrange the pear pieces on top, then sprinkle over the ginger. Cover with the potatoes. Pour in the cider and season to taste with salt and pepper. Cover and cook in the preheated oven for 1¼ hours.

3 Trim the stem ends of the green beans and cut in half. Remove the casserole from the oven and add the beans, then re-cover and return to the oven for an additional 30 minutes. Taste and adjust the seasoning and sprinkle with the chives. Serve immediately.

Pot-Roast Pork

INGREDIENTS

serves ❹

1 tbsp corn oil

4 tbsp butter

2 lb 4 oz/1 kg boned and rolled pork loin

4 shallots, chopped

6 juniper berries

2 fresh thyme sprigs, plus extra to garnish

⅔ cup hard cider

⅔ cup chicken stock or water

8 celery stalks, chopped

2 tbsp all-purpose flour

⅔ cup heavy cream

salt and pepper

freshly cooked peas, to serve

1 Heat the oil with half the butter in a heavy-bottom pan or flameproof casserole. Add the pork and cook over medium heat, turning frequently, for 5–10 minutes, or until browned. Transfer to a plate.

2 Add the shallots to the pan and cook, stirring frequently, for 5 minutes, or until softened. Add the juniper berries and thyme sprigs and return the pork to the pan, with any juices that have collected on the plate. Pour in the cider and stock, season to taste with salt and pepper, then cover and simmer for 30 minutes. Turn the pork over and add the celery. Re-cover the pan and cook for an additional 40 minutes.

3 Meanwhile, make a beurre manié by mashing the remaining butter with the flour in a small bowl. Transfer the pork and celery to a platter with a slotted spoon and keep warm. Remove and discard the juniper berries and thyme. Whisk the beurre manié, a little at a time, into the simmering cooking liquid. Cook, stirring constantly, for 2 minutes, then stir in the cream and bring to a boil.

4 Slice the pork and spoon a little of the sauce over it. Garnish with thyme sprigs and serve immediately with the celery, peas, and remaining sauce.

Pork with Red Cabbage

INGREDIENTS

1 tbsp corn oil

1 lb 10 oz/750 g boned and rolled pork loin

1 onion, finely chopped

1 lb 2 oz/500 g red cabbage, thick stems removed and leaves shredded

2 large cooking apples, peeled, cored, and sliced

3 cloves

1 tsp brown sugar

3 tbsp lemon juice, and a thinly pared strip of lemon rind

lemon wedges, to garnish

serves ❹

1 Preheat the oven to 325°F/160°C. Heat the oil in a flameproof casserole. Add the pork and cook over medium heat, turning frequently, for 5–10 minutes, until browned. Transfer to a plate.

2 Add the chopped onion to the casserole and cook over low heat, stirring occasionally, for 5 minutes, or until softened. Add the cabbage, in batches, and cook, stirring, for 2 minutes. Transfer each batch (mixed with some onion) into a bowl with a slotted spoon.

3 Add the apple slices, cloves, and sugar to the bowl and mix well, then place about half the mixture in the bottom of the casserole. Top with the pork and add the remaining cabbage mixture. Sprinkle in the lemon juice and add the strip of rind. Cover and cook in the preheated oven for 1½ hours.

4 Transfer the pork to a plate. Transfer the cabbage mixture to the plate with a slotted spoon and keep warm. Bring the cooking juices to a boil over high heat and reduce slightly. Slice the pork and arrange on warmed serving plates, surrounded with the cabbage mixture. Spoon the cooking juices over the meat and serve with wedges of lemon.

Rice & Peas

INGREDIENTS

1 tbsp olive oil

4 tbsp butter

2 oz/55 g pancetta or fatty bacon, chopped

1 small onion, chopped

6¼ cups hot chicken stock

1 cup risotto rice

3 tbsp chopped fresh parsley

2 cup frozen peas

½ cup freshly grated Parmesan cheese

pepper

serves **4**

1 Heat the olive oil and half of the butter in a heavy-bottom pan. Add the pancetta or bacon and onion and cook over low heat, stirring occasionally, for 5 minutes, until the onion is softened and translucent, but not browned.

2 Add the stock to the pan and bring to a boil. Stir in the rice and season to taste with pepper. Bring to a boil, lower the heat, and simmer, stirring occasionally, for 20–30 minutes, until the rice is tender.

3 Add the parsley and the peas and cook for about 8 minutes, until the peas are heated through. Stir in the remaining butter and the Parmesan.

4 Transfer to a warmed serving dish and serve immediately with freshly ground black pepper.

Potato & Sausage Pan-Fry

INGREDIENTS

serves ❹

1½ lb/675 g potatoes, cubed

2 tbsp butter

8 large herb sausages

4 smoked bacon slices

1 onion, quartered

1 zucchini, sliced

⅔ cup dry white wine

1¼ cups vegetable bouillon

1 tsp Worcestershire sauce

2 tbsp chopped mixed fresh herbs

salt and pepper

chopped fresh herbs, to garnish

1 Cook the cubed potatoes in a saucepan of boiling water for 10 minutes, or until softened. Drain thoroughly and set aside.

2 Melt the butter in a large skillet. Add the sausages and cook for 5 minutes, turning them frequently to ensure that they brown on all sides.

3 Add the bacon slices, onion, zucchini and potatoes to the pan. Cook the mixture for another 10 minutes, stirring the mixture and turning the sausages frequently.

4 Stir in the white wine, bouillon, Worcestershire sauce, and chopped mixed herbs. Season with salt and pepper to taste and cook the mixture over gentle heat for 10 minutes. Add more salt and pepper, if necessary.

5 Transfer the potato and sausage pan-fry to warm serving plates, garnish with chopped fresh herbs, and serve at once.

2 Poultry

Versatile chicken forms the basis of a
wealth of one-pot meals—from the classic
French coq au vin to spicy Asian curries.
Turkey takes on a new lease of life in a
speedy one-pan stir-fry with cranberries,
or try it Mexican-style with chiles. Sweet
and meaty duck goes into a fragrant
one-pot Asian braise, or a sweet-sharp
Mediterranean-style stew with olives.
The possibilities are endless—all you need
is a pot.

Chicken & Barley Stew

INGREDIENTS

serves 4

2 tbsp vegetable oil

8 small, skinless chicken thighs

generous 2 cups chicken stock

scant ½ cup pearl barley, rinsed and drained

7 oz/200 g small new potatoes, scrubbed and cut in half lengthwise

2 large carrots, peeled and sliced

1 leek, trimmed and sliced

2 shallots, sliced

1 tbsp tomato paste

1 bay leaf

1 zucchini, trimmed and sliced

2 tbsp chopped fresh flat-leaf parsley, plus extra sprigs to garnish

2 tbsp all-purpose flour

salt and pepper

fresh crusty bread, to serve

1 Heat the oil in a large pot over medium heat. Add the chicken and cook for 3 minutes, then turn over and cook on the other side for another 2 minutes. Add the stock, barley, potatoes, carrots, leek, shallots, tomato paste, and bay leaf. Bring to a boil, lower the heat, and simmer for 30 minutes.

2 Add the zucchini and chopped parsley, cover the pan, and cook for another 20 minutes, or until the chicken is cooked through. Remove the bay leaf and discard.

3 In a separate bowl, mix the flour with 4 tablespoons of water and stir into a smooth paste. Add it to the stew and cook, stirring, over low heat for another 5 minutes. Season to taste with salt and pepper.

4 Remove from the heat, ladle into individual serving bowls, and garnish with sprigs of fresh parsley. Serve with fresh crusty bread.

Coq au Vin

INGREDIENTS

serves 4

¼ cup butter

2 tbsp olive oil

4 lb/1.8 kg chicken pieces

4 oz/115 g rindless smoked bacon, cut into strips

4 oz/115 g pearl onions, peeled

4 oz/115 g cremini mushrooms, halved

2 garlic cloves, finely chopped

2 tbsp brandy

scant 1 cup red wine

1¼ cups chicken stock

1 bouquet garni

salt and pepper

2 tbsp all-purpose flour

bay leaves, to garnish

1 Melt half the butter with the olive oil in a large, flameproof casserole. Add the chicken and cook over medium heat, stirring, for 8–10 minutes, or until golden brown. Add the bacon, onions, mushrooms, and garlic.

2 Pour in the brandy and set it alight with a match or taper. When the flames have died down, add the wine, stock, and bouquet garni and season to taste with salt and pepper. Bring to a boil, reduce the heat, and simmer gently for 1 hour, or until the chicken pieces are cooked through and tender. Meanwhile, make a beurre manié by mashing the remaining butter with the flour in a small bowl.

3 Remove and discard the bouquet garni. Transfer the chicken to a large plate and keep warm. Stir the beurre manié into the casserole, a little at a time. Bring to a boil, return the chicken to the casserole, and serve immediately, garnished with bay leaves.

Italian-Style Roast Chicken

INGREDIENTS

5 lb 8 oz/2.5 kg chicken

sprigs of fresh rosemary

¾ cup feta cheese, coarsely grated

2 tbsp sun-dried tomato paste

4 tbsp butter, softened

1 bulb garlic

2 lb 4 oz/1 kg new potatoes, halved if large

1 each red, green, and yellow bell pepper, seeded and cut into chunks

3 zucchini, sliced thinly

2 tbsp olive oil

salt and pepper

1¼ cups prepared gravy

serves 6

1 Preheat the oven to 375°F/190°C. Rinse the chicken inside and out with cold water and drain well. Carefully cut between the skin and the top of the breast meat using a small pointed knife. Slide a finger into the slit and carefully enlarge it to form a pocket. Continue until the skin is completely lifted away from both breasts and the top of the legs.

2 Chop the leaves from 3 rosemary stems. Mix with the feta cheese, sun-dried tomato paste, butter, and pepper to taste, then spoon under the skin. Put the chicken in a large roasting pan, cover with foil, and cook for 20 minutes per 1 lb 2 oz/500 g, plus 20 minutes.

3 Break the garlic bulb into cloves but do not peel. Add the vegetables and garlic to the chicken after 40 minutes.

4 Drizzle with oil, tuck in a few stems of rosemary, and season with salt and pepper. Cook for the remaining calculated time, removing the foil for the last 40 minutes to brown the chicken. Serve immediately with the vegetables and the gravy.

Spicy Aromatic Chicken

INGREDIENTS

serves ❹

4–8 chicken pieces, skinned

½ lemon, cut into wedges

4 tbsp olive oil

1 onion, chopped coarsely

2 large garlic cloves,
chopped finely

½ cup dry white wine

14 oz/400 g canned chopped
tomatoes, with their juice

pinch of sugar

½ tsp ground cinnamon

½ tsp ground cloves

½ tsp ground allspice

14 oz/400 g canned artichoke
hearts or okra, drained

8 black olives, pitted

salt and pepper

1 Rub the chicken pieces with the lemon. Heat the oil in a large flameproof casserole or lidded skillet. Add the onion and garlic and fry for 5 minutes, until softened. Add the chicken pieces and fry for 5–10 minutes, until browned on all sides.

2 Pour in the wine and add the tomatoes with their juice, the sugar, cinnamon, cloves, allspice, salt and pepper to taste, and bring to a boil. Cover the casserole and simmer for 45 minutes to 1 hour, until the chicken is tender.

3 Meanwhile, if using artichoke hearts, cut them in half. Add the artichokes or okra and the olives to the casserole 10 minutes before the end of cooking, and continue to simmer until heated through. Serve hot.

Chicken in White Wine

INGREDIENTS

serves 4

4 tbsp butter

2 tbsp olive oil

2 thick, rindless, lean bacon strips, chopped

4 oz/115 g pearl onions, peeled

1 garlic clove, finely chopped

4 lb/1.8 kg chicken pieces

1¾ cups dry white wine

1¼ cups chicken stock

1 bouquet garni

4 oz/115 g button mushrooms

2½ tbsp all-purpose flour

salt and pepper

fresh mixed herbs, to garnish

1 Preheat the oven to 325°F/160°C. Melt half the butter with the oil in a flameproof casserole. Add the bacon and cook over medium heat, stirring, for 5–10 minutes, or until golden brown. Transfer the bacon to a large plate. Add the onions and garlic to the casserole and cook over low heat, stirring occasionally, for 10 minutes, or until golden. Transfer to the plate. Add the chicken and cook over medium heat, stirring constantly, for 8–10 minutes, or until golden. Transfer to the plate.

2 Drain off any excess fat from the casserole. Stir in the wine and stock and bring to a boil, scraping any sediment off the bottom. Add the bouquet garni and season to taste. Return the bacon, onions, and chicken to the casserole. Cover and cook in the preheated oven for 1 hour. Add the mushrooms, re-cover, and cook for 15 minutes. Meanwhile, make a beurre manié by mashing the remaining butter with the flour in a small bowl.

3 Remove the casserole from the oven and set over medium heat. Remove and discard the bouquet garni. Whisk in the beurre manié, a little at a time. Bring to a boil, stirring constantly, then serve, garnished with fresh herb sprigs.

Florida Chicken

INGREDIENTS

serves 4

1 lb/450 g skinless, boneless chicken

1½ tbsp all-purpose flour

1 tbsp olive oil

1 onion, cut into wedges

2 celery stalks, sliced

⅔ cup orange juice

1¼ cups chicken stock

1 tbsp light soy sauce

1–2 tsp clear honey

1 tbsp grated orange rind

1 orange bell pepper, seeded and chopped

8 oz/225 g zucchini, sliced into semicircles

2 small corn cobs, halved, or 3½ oz/100 g baby corn

1 orange, peeled and segmented

salt and pepper

1 tbsp chopped fresh parsley, to garnish

1 Lightly rinse the chicken and pat dry with paper towels. Cut into bite-size pieces. Season the flour well with salt and pepper. Toss the chicken in the seasoned flour until well coated and reserve any remaining seasoned flour.

2 Heat the oil in a large, heavy-bottom skillet and cook the chicken over high heat, stirring frequently, for 5 minutes, or until golden on all sides and sealed. Using a slotted spoon, transfer to a plate.

3 Add the onion and celery to the skillet and cook over medium heat, stirring frequently, for 5 minutes, or until softened. Sprinkle in the reserved seasoned flour and cook, stirring constantly, for 2 minutes, then remove from the heat. Gradually stir in the orange juice, stock, soy sauce, and honey followed by the orange rind, then return to the heat and bring to a boil, stirring.

4 Return the chicken to the skillet. Reduce the heat, then cover and simmer, stirring occasionally, for 15 minutes. Add the orange bell pepper, zucchini, and corn cobs and simmer for an additional 10 minutes, or until the chicken and vegetables are tender. Add the orange segments, then stir well and heat through for 1 minute. Serve garnished with the parsley.

Thai Green Chicken Curry

INGREDIENTS

2 tbsp peanut or corn oil

2 tbsp prepared green curry paste

1 lb 2 oz/500 g skinless boneless chicken breasts, cut into cubes

2 kaffir lime leaves, coarsely torn

1 lemongrass stalk, finely chopped

1 cup canned coconut milk

16 baby eggplants, halved

2 tbsp Thai fish sauce

fresh Thai basil sprigs, to garnish

kaffir lime leaves, thinly sliced, to garnish

serves ❹

1 Heat the oil in a preheated wok or large, heavy-bottom skillet. Add the curry paste and stir-fry briefly until all the aromas are released.

2 Add the chicken, lime leaves, and lemongrass and stir-fry for 3–4 minutes, until the meat is starting to color. Add the coconut milk and eggplants and let simmer gently for 8–10 minutes, or until tender.

3 Stir in the fish sauce and serve at once, garnished with Thai basil sprigs and lime leaves.

Chicken Jalfrezi

INGREDIENTS

serves 4

½ tsp cumin seeds

½ tsp coriander seeds

1 tsp mustard oil

3 tbsp vegetable oil

1 large onion, finely chopped

3 garlic cloves, crushed

1 tbsp tomato paste

2 tomatoes, peeled and chopped

1 tsp ground turmeric

½ tsp chili powder

½ tsp garam masala

1 tsp red wine vinegar

1 small red bell pepper, seeded and chopped

4½ oz/125 g frozen fava beans

1 lb 2 oz/500 g cooked chicken, chopped

salt

fresh cilantro sprigs, to garnish

freshly cooked rice, to serve

1 Grind the cumin and coriander seeds in a mortar with a pestle, then reserve. Heat the mustard oil in a large, heavy-bottom skillet over high heat for 1 minute, or until it begins to smoke. Add the vegetable oil, reduce the heat, and add the onion and garlic. Cook for 10 minutes, or until golden.

2 Add the tomato paste, chopped tomatoes, turmeric, ground cumin and coriander seeds, chili powder, garam masala, and vinegar to the skillet. Stir the mixture until fragrant.

3 Add the red bell pepper and fava beans and stir for an additional 2 minutes, or until the bell pepper is softened. Stir in the chicken, and season to taste with salt, then simmer gently for 6–8 minutes, until the chicken is heated through and the beans are tender. Transfer to warmed serving bowls, garnish with cilantro sprigs, and serve with freshly cooked rice.

Chicken Pepperonata

INGREDIENTS

serves 4

8 skinless chicken thighs

2 tbsp whole wheat flour

2 tbsp olive oil

1 small onion, sliced thinly

1 garlic clove, crushed

1 each large red, yellow, and green bell peppers, seeded and thinly sliced

14 oz/400 g can chopped tomatoes

1 tbsp chopped fresh oregano, plus extra to garnish

salt and pepper

crusty whole wheat bread, to serve

1 Toss the chicken thighs in the flour, shaking off the excess.

2 Heat the oil in a wide skillet and fry the chicken quickly until sealed and lightly browned, then remove from the pan.

3 Add the onion to the pan and gently fry until soft. Add the garlic, bell peppers, tomatoes, and oregano, then bring to a boil, stirring.

4 Arrange the chicken over the vegetables, season well with salt and pepper, then cover the pan tightly and simmer for 20–25 minutes, or until the chicken is completely cooked and tender.

5 Taste and adjust the seasoning if necessary, garnish with oregano, and serve with crusty whole wheat bread.

Chicken Risotto with Saffron

INGREDIENTS

serves 4

generous ½ cup butter

2 lb/900 g skinless, boneless chicken breasts, thinly sliced

1 large onion, chopped

1 lb 2 oz/500 g risotto rice

⅔ cup white wine

1 tsp crumbled saffron threads

generous 5½ cups boiling chicken stock

salt and pepper

½ cup freshly grated Parmesan cheese

1 Melt 4 tablespoons of the butter in a deep pan, add the chicken and onion and cook, stirring frequently, for 8 minutes, or until golden brown.

2 Add the rice and mix to coat in the butter. Cook, stirring constantly for 2–3 minutes, or until the grains are translucent. Add the wine and cook, stirring constantly, for 1 minute until reduced.

3 Mix the saffron with 4 tablespoons of the hot stock. Add the liquid to the rice and cook, stirring constantly, until it is absorbed.

4 Gradually add the remaining hot stock, a ladleful at a time. Stir constantly and add more liquid as the rice absorbs each addition. Cook for 20 minutes, or until all the liquid is absorbed and the rice is creamy. Season to taste.

5 Remove the risotto from the heat and add the remaining butter. Mix well, then stir in the Parmesan until it melts. Spoon the risotto onto warmed plates and serve at once.

Mexican Turkey

INGREDIENTS

6 tbsp all-purpose flour

4 turkey breast fillets

3 tbsp corn oil

1 onion, thinly sliced

1 red bell pepper, seeded and sliced

1¼ cups chicken stock

2 tbsp raisins

4 tomatoes, peeled, seeded, and chopped

1 tsp chili powder

½ tsp ground cinnamon

pinch of ground cumin

1 oz/25 g semisweet chocolate, finely chopped or grated

salt and pepper

sprigs of fresh cilantro, to garnish

serves ❹

1 Preheat the oven to 325°F/160°C. Spread the flour on a plate and season with salt and pepper. Coat the turkey fillets in the seasoned flour, shaking off any excess.

2 Heat the oil in a flameproof casserole. Add the turkey fillets and cook over medium heat, turning occasionally, for 5–10 minutes, or until golden. Transfer to a plate with a slotted spoon.

3 Add the onion and bell pepper to the casserole. Cook over low heat, stirring occasionally, for 5 minutes, or until softened. Sprinkle in any remaining seasoned flour and cook, stirring constantly, for 1 minute. Gradually stir in the stock, then add the raisins, chopped tomatoes, chili powder, cinnamon, cumin, and chocolate. Season to taste with salt and pepper. Bring to a boil, stirring constantly.

4 Return the turkey to the casserole, cover, and cook in the preheated oven for 50 minutes. Serve immediately, garnished with sprigs of cilantro.

Italian Turkey Steaks

INGREDIENTS

serves ❹

1 tbsp olive oil

4 turkey scallops or steaks

2 red bell peppers

1 red onion

2 garlic cloves, finely chopped

1¼ cups strained tomatoes

⅔ cup medium white wine

1 tbsp chopped fresh marjoram

14 oz/400 g canned cannellini beans, drained and rinsed

3 tbsp fresh white breadcrumbs

salt and pepper

fresh basil sprigs, to garnish

1 Heat the oil in a flameproof casserole or heavy-bottom skillet. Add the turkey scallops and cook over medium heat for 5–10 minutes, turning occasionally, until golden. Transfer to a plate.

2 Seed and slice the red bell peppers. Slice the onion, add to the skillet with the bell peppers, and cook over low heat, stirring occasionally, for 5 minutes, or until softened. Add the garlic and cook for an additional 2 minutes. Return the turkey to the skillet and add the strained tomatoes, wine, and marjoram. Season to taste. Bring to a boil, then reduce the heat, cover, and simmer, stirring occasionally, for 25–30 minutes, or until the turkey is cooked through and tender.

3 Stir in the cannellini beans. Simmer for an additional 5 minutes. Sprinkle the breadcrumbs over the top and place under a preheated medium-hot broiler for 2–3 minutes, or until golden. Serve, garnished with basil.

Turkey in a Piquant Sauce

INGREDIENTS

2 tbsp all-purpose flour

2 lb 4 oz/1 kg turkey pieces

2 tbsp butter

1 tbsp corn oil

2 onions, sliced

1 garlic clove, finely chopped

1 red bell pepper, seeded and sliced

14 oz/400 g canned chopped tomatoes, with their juice

1 sprig rosemary

⅔ cup chicken stock

salt and pepper

2 tbsp chopped fresh parsley, to garnish

serves ❹

1 Spread the flour on a plate and season with salt and pepper. Coat the turkey pieces in the seasoned flour, shaking off any excess.

2 Melt the butter with the oil in a flameproof casserole or large pan. Add the turkey and cook over medium heat, stirring, for 5–10 minutes, or until golden. Transfer the turkey pieces to a plate with a slotted spoon and keep warm.

3 Add the onions, garlic, and bell pepper to the casserole and cook, stirring occasionally, for 5 minutes, or until softened. Sprinkle in any remaining flour and cook, stirring constantly, for 1 minute. Return the turkey pieces to the casserole, then add the tomatoes and their juice, the rosemary, and stock. Bring to a boil, stirring constantly, then cover and simmer for 1¼ hours, or until the turkey is cooked through and tender.

4 Transfer the turkey to a serving platter with a slotted spoon. Remove and discard the rosemary. Return the sauce to a boil and cook until reduced and thickened. Season to taste with salt and pepper and pour over the turkey. Serve immediately, garnished with parsley.

Stir-Fried Turkey with Cranberry Glaze

INGREDIENTS

1 lb/450 g boneless turkey breast

2 tbsp corn oil

2 tbsp preserved ginger

½ cup fresh or frozen cranberries

3½ oz/100 g canned chestnuts

4 tbsp cranberry sauce

3 tbsp light soy sauce

salt and pepper

serves ❹

1 Remove any skin from the turkey breast and, using a sharp knife, thinly slice the meat.

2 Heat the corn oil in a large preheated wok or heavy skillet. .

3 Add the slices of turkey to the wok or skillet and stir-fry over medium heat for about 5 minutes, or until cooked through.

4 Drain the preserved ginger in a small strainer, then, using a sharp knife, chop finely.

5 Add the preserved ginger and the cranberries to the wok or skillet and cook for 2–3 minutes, or until the cranberries have started to become soft.

6 Add the chestnuts, cranberry sauce, and soy sauce, season to taste with salt and pepper, and bubble for 2–3 minutes.

7 Transfer the glazed turkey stir-fry to warmed individual serving dishes and serve immediately.

Orange Turkey with Rice

INGREDIENTS

1 tbsp olive oil

1 medium onion, chopped

1 lb/450 g skinless lean turkey (such as fillet), cut into thin strips

1¼ cups unsweetened orange juice

1 bay leaf

3 cups small broccoli florets

1 large zucchini, diced

1 large orange

6 cups cooked brown rice

salt and pepper

tomato and onion salad, to serve

9–10 pitted black olives in brine, drained and quartered, to garnish

shredded basil leaves, to garnish

serves ❹

1 Heat the oil in a large skillet and cook the onion and turkey, stirring, for 4–5 minutes, until lightly browned.

2 Pour in the orange juice and add the bay leaf and seasoning. Bring to a boil and simmer for 10 minutes.

3 Meanwhile, bring a large pan of water to a boil and cook the broccoli florets, covered, for 2 minutes. Add the diced zucchini, then bring back to a boil. Cover and cook for another 3 minutes. Drain and set aside.

4 Using a sharp knife, peel off the skin and white pith from the orange. Slice down the orange to make thin circular slices, then halve each slice.

5 Stir the broccoli, zucchini, rice, and orange slices into the turkey mixture. Gently mix together and season, then heat through for another 3–4 minutes, or until the mixture is piping hot.

6 Transfer the turkey rice to warm serving plates and garnish with black olives and shredded basil leaves. Serve with a fresh tomato and onion salad.

Duck Legs with Olives

INGREDIENTS

serves 4

4 duck legs, all visible fat trimmed off

1 lb 12 oz/800 g canned tomatoes, chopped

8 garlic cloves, peeled, but left whole

1 large onion, chopped

1 carrot, peeled and chopped finely

1 celery stalk, peeled and chopped finely

3 sprigs fresh thyme

generous ½ cup Spanish green olives in brine, stuffed with pimientos, garlic, or almonds, drained and rinsed

1 tsp finely grated orange rind

salt and pepper

1 Put the duck legs in the bottom of a flameproof casserole or a large, heavy-bottom skillet with a tight-fitting lid. Add the tomatoes, garlic, onion, carrot, celery, thyme, and olives, and stir together. Season with salt and pepper to taste.

2 Turn the heat to high and cook, uncovered, until the ingredients start to bubble. Reduce the heat to low, cover tightly, and let simmer for 1¼–1½ hours, until the duck is very tender. Check occasionally and add a little water if the mixture appears to be drying out.

3 When the duck is tender, transfer it to a serving platter, cover, and keep hot in a preheated warm oven. Leave the casserole uncovered, increase the heat to medium, and cook, stirring, for about 10 minutes, until the mixture forms a sauce. Stir in the orange rind, then taste and adjust the seasoning if necessary.

4 Mash the tender garlic cloves with a fork and spread over the duck legs. Spoon the sauce over the top. Serve at once.

Braised Asian Duck

INGREDIENTS

3 tbsp soy sauce

¼ tsp Chinese five-spice powder

4 duck legs or breasts, cut into pieces

3 tbsp vegetable oil

1 tsp dark sesame oil

1 tsp finely chopped fresh ginger

1 large garlic clove, finely chopped

4 scallions, white part thickly sliced, green part shredded

2 tbsp rice wine or dry sherry

1 tbsp oyster sauce

3 whole star anise

2 tsp black peppercorns

2–2½ cups chicken stock or water

8 oz/225 g canned water chestnuts, drained

2 tbsp cornstarch

salt and pepper

serves ❹

1 Combine 1 tablespoon of the soy sauce, the five-spice powder, salt and pepper to taste and rub over the duck pieces. Heat 2½ tablespoons of the vegetable oil in a flameproof casserole, add the duck pieces, and cook over a medium heat, stirring, until browned. Transfer to a plate with a slotted spoon.

2 Drain the fat from the casserole and wipe out with paper towels. Heat the sesame oil and remaining vegetable oil. Add the ginger and garlic. Cook for a few seconds. Add the white scallions. Cook for a few seconds. Return the duck to the pan. Add the rice wine, oyster sauce, star anise, peppercorns, and remaining soy sauce. Pour in just enough stock to cover and add the water chestnuts. Bring to a boil, cover, and simmer gently for 1½ hours, adding more water if necessary.

3 Mix the cornstarch with 2 tablespoons of the cooking liquid to a smooth paste. Add to the remaining liquid, stirring until thickened. Garnish with the green scallion shreds to serve.

3 Fish & Seafood

Fish and seafood make mouthwatering one-pot soups and stews. Try firm-fleshed chunks of white fish and plump juicy mussels and shrimp in French bouillabaise or a Moroccan fish tagine. Equally delicious are seafood and rice, easily cooked from start to finish in a wide deep pan. For maximum flavor try baking firm-fleshed fish in the simplest container of all, a sealed paper or foil package that retains every bit of flavor.

Bouillabaisse

INGREDIENTS

serves ❹

7 oz/200 g live mussels

scant ½ cup olive oil

3 garlic cloves, chopped

2 onions, chopped

2 tomatoes, seeded and chopped

generous 2¾ cups fish stock

1¾ cups white wine

1 bay leaf

pinch of saffron threads

2 tbsp chopped fresh basil

2 tbsp chopped fresh parsley

9 oz/250 g snapper or monkfish fillets

9 oz/250 g haddock fillets, skinned

7 oz/200 g shrimp, peeled and deveined

3½ oz/100 g scallops

salt and pepper

fresh baguettes, to serve

1 Soak the mussels in lightly salted water for 10 minutes. Scrub the shells under cold running water and pull off any beards. Discard any with broken shells. Tap the remaining mussels and discard any that refuse to close. Put the rest into a large pan with a little water, bring to a boil, and cook over high heat for 4 minutes. Transfer the cooked mussels to a bowl, discarding any that remain closed, and reserve. Wipe out the pan with paper towels.

2 Heat the oil in the pan over medium heat. Add the garlic and onions and cook, stirring, for 3 minutes. Stir in the tomatoes, stock, wine, bay leaf, saffron, and herbs. Bring to a boil, reduce the heat, cover, and simmer for 30 minutes.

3 When the tomato mixture is cooked, rinse the fish, pat dry, and cut into chunks. Add to the pan and simmer for 5 minutes. Add the mussels, shrimp, and scallops, and season. Cook for 3 minutes, until the fish is cooked through.

4 Remove from the heat, discard the bay leaf, and ladle into serving bowls. Serve with fresh baguettes.

Mediterranean Fish Stew

INGREDIENTS

serves **4**

2 tbsp olive oil

1 onion, sliced

pinch of saffron threads, lightly crushed

1 tbsp chopped fresh thyme

2 garlic cloves, finely chopped

1 lb 12 oz/800 g canned chopped tomatoes, drained

8 cups fish stock

¾ cup dry white wine

12 oz/350 g red snapper or pompano fillets, cut into chunks

1 lb/450 g monkfish fillet, cut into chunks

1 lb/450 g fresh clams, scrubbed

8 oz/225 g squid rings

salt and pepper

2 tbsp fresh basil leaves, plus extra to garnish

1 Heat the oil in a large, flameproof casserole. Add the onion, saffron, thyme, and a pinch of salt. Cook over low heat, stirring occasionally, for 5 minutes, or until the onion has softened.

2 Add the garlic and cook for an additional 2 minutes, then add the drained tomatoes and pour in the stock and wine. Season to taste with salt and pepper, bring the mixture to a boil, then reduce the heat and simmer for 15 minutes.

3 Add the chunks of red snapper and monkfish and simmer for 3 minutes. Add the clams and squid and simmer for 5 minutes, or until the clam shells have opened. Discard any clams that remain closed. Tear in the basil and stir. Serve garnished with the extra basil leaves.

Seafood in Saffron Sauce

INGREDIENTS

serves 4

8 oz/225 g live mussels

8 oz/225 g live clams

2 tbsp olive oil

1 onion, sliced

pinch of saffron threads

1 tbsp chopped fresh thyme

2 garlic cloves, finely chopped

1 lb 12 oz/800 g canned tomatoes, drained and chopped

¾ cup dry white wine

8 cups fish stock

12 oz/350 g red snapper fillets, cut into bite-size chunks

1 lb/450 g monkfish fillet, cut into bite-size chunks

8 oz/225 g raw squid rings

2 tbsp fresh shredded basil leaves

salt and pepper

fresh bread, to serve

1 Clean the mussels and clams by scrubbing or scraping the shells and pulling out any beards that are attached to the mussels. Discard any with broken shells or any that refuse to close when tapped.

2 Heat the oil in a large, flameproof casserole and cook the onion with the saffron, thyme, and a pinch of salt over low heat, stirring occasionally, for 5 minutes, or until softened.

3 Add the garlic and cook, stirring, for 2 minutes. Add the tomatoes, wine, and stock, then season to taste with salt and pepper and stir well. Bring to a boil, then reduce the heat and simmer for 15 minutes.

4 Add the fish chunks and simmer for an additional 3 minutes. Add the clams, mussels, and squid rings and simmer for an additional 5 minutes, or until the mussels and clams have opened. Discard any that remain closed. Stir in the basil and serve immediately, accompanied by plenty of fresh bread to mop up the broth.

Moroccan Fish Tagine

INGREDIENTS

serves 4

2 tbsp olive oil

1 large onion, finely chopped

pinch of saffron threads

½ tsp ground cinnamon

1 tsp ground coriander

½ tsp ground cumin

½ tsp ground turmeric

7 oz/200 g canned chopped tomatoes

1¼ cups fish stock

4 small red snappers, cleaned, boned, and heads and tails removed

2 oz/55 g pitted green olives

1 tbsp chopped preserved lemon

3 tbsp chopped fresh cilantro

salt and pepper

freshly cooked couscous, to serve

1 Heat the olive oil in a flameproof casserole. Add the onion and cook gently over very low heat, stirring occasionally, for 10 minutes, or until softened, but not colored. Add the saffron, cinnamon, ground coriander, cumin, and turmeric and cook for an additional 30 seconds, stirring constantly.

2 Add the tomatoes and fish stock and stir well. Bring to a boil, reduce the heat, cover, and simmer for 15 minutes. Uncover and simmer for 20–35 minutes, or until thickened.

3 Cut each red snapper in half, then add the fish pieces to the casserole, pushing them down into the liquid. Simmer the stew for an additional 5–6 minutes, or until the fish is just cooked.

4 Carefully stir in the olives, lemon, and fresh cilantro. Season to taste with salt and pepper and serve immediately with couscous.

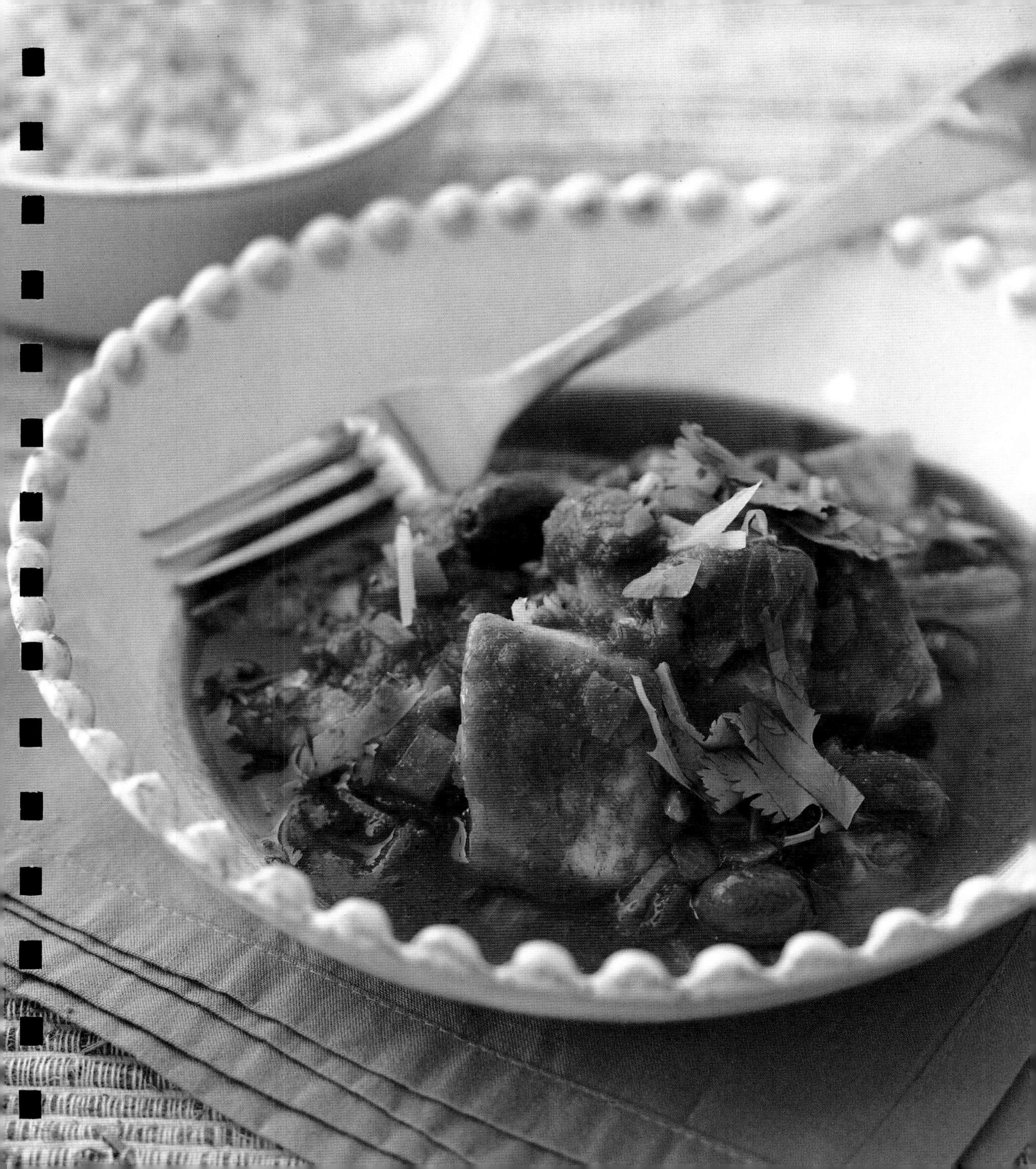

Moules Marinières

INGREDIENTS

serves 4

4 lb 8 oz/2 kg live mussels

1¼ cups dry white wine

6 shallots, finely chopped

1 bouquet garni

pepper

crusty bread, to serve

1 Clean the mussels by scrubbing or scraping the shells and pulling off any beards. Discard any with broken shells or any that refuse to close when tapped with a knife. Rinse the mussels under cold running water.

2 Pour the wine into a large, heavy-bottom pan, add the shallots and bouquet garni, and season to taste with pepper. Bring to a boil over medium heat. Add the mussels, cover tightly, and cook, shaking the pan occasionally, for 5 minutes. Remove and discard the bouquet garni and any mussels that remain closed.

3 Strain the cooking liquid through a cheesecloth-lined strainer, then return to a clean saucepan and reheat. Divide the mussels among 4 soup bowls with a slotted spoon. Spoon the hot cooking liquid over the mussels and serve immediately with bread.

Squid with Parsley & Pine Kernels

INGREDIENTS

serves **4**

½ cup golden raisins

5 tbsp olive oil

2 tbsp chopped fresh flat-leaf parsley, plus extra to garnish

2 garlic cloves, finely chopped

1 lb 12 oz/800 g prepared squid, sliced, or squid rings

½ cup dry white wine

1 lb 2 oz/500 g strained tomatoes

pinch of chili powder

pinch of salt

¾ cup pine nuts, finely chopped

1 Place the golden raisins in a small bowl, cover with lukewarm water, and set aside for 15 minutes to plump up.

2 Meanwhile, heat the olive oil in a heavy-bottom pan. Add the parsley and garlic and cook over low heat, stirring frequently, for 3 minutes. Add the squid and cook, stirring occasionally, for 5 minutes.

3 Increase the heat to medium, pour in the wine, and cook until it has almost completely evaporated. Stir in the strained tomatoes and season to taste with chili powder and salt. Reduce the heat again, cover, and let simmer gently, stirring occasionally, for 45–50 minutes, until the squid is almost tender.

4 Drain the golden raisins and stir them into the pan with the pine nuts. Let simmer for an additional 10 minutes, then serve immediately garnished with the reserved chopped parsley.

Jambalaya

INGREDIENTS

serves ❹

2 tbsp vegetable oil

1 green bell pepper, seeded and coarsely chopped

2 celery stalks, coarsely chopped

3 garlic cloves, finely chopped

2 tsp paprika

10½ oz/300 g skinless, boneless chicken breasts, chopped

3½ oz/100 g boudin sausages, chopped

3 tomatoes, peeled and chopped

2 cups long-grain rice

3¾ cups hot chicken or fish stock

1 tsp dried oregano

2 bay leaves

12 large jumbo shrimp

2 tbsp chopped fresh parsley

salt and pepper

1 Heat the vegetable oil in a large skillet over low heat. Add the bell pepper, celery, and garlic and cook for 8–10 minutes, until all the vegetables have softened. Add the paprika and cook for another 30 seconds. Add the chicken and sausages and cook for 8–10 minutes, until lightly browned. Add the tomatoes and cook for 2–3 minutes, until they have collapsed.

2 Add the rice to the pan and stir well. Pour in the hot stock, oregano, and bay leaves and stir well. Cover and let simmer for 10 minutes.

3 Add the shrimp and stir well. Cover again and cook for another 6–8 minutes, until the rice is tender and the shrimp are cooked through.

4 Stir in the parsley, and season to taste with salt and pepper. Transfer to a large serving dish and serve.

Shrimp with Coconut Rice

INGREDIENTS

serves **4**

1 cup dried Chinese mushrooms

2 tbsp vegetable or peanut oil

6 scallions, chopped

scant ½ cup dry unsweetened shredded coconut

1 fresh green chile, seeded and chopped

heaping 1 cup jasmine rice

⅔ cup fish stock

1¾ cups coconut milk

12 oz/350 g cooked shelled shrimp

6 sprigs fresh Thai basil

1 Place the mushrooms in a small bowl, cover with hot water, and set aside to soak for 30 minutes. Drain, then cut off and discard the stalks and slice the caps.

2 Heat the oil in a wok and stir-fry the scallions, coconut, and chile for 2–3 minutes, until lightly browned. Add the mushrooms and stir-fry for 3–4 minutes.

3 Add the rice and stir-fry for 2–3 minutes, then add the stock and bring to a boil. Reduce the heat and add the coconut milk. Let simmer for 10–15 minutes, until the rice is tender. Stir in the shrimp and basil, heat through, and serve.

Seafood Risotto

INGREDIENTS

serves 4

1 tbsp olive oil

4 tbsp butter

2 garlic cloves, chopped

1¾ cups risotto rice

generous 5½ cups boiling fish or chicken stock

9 oz/250 g mixed cooked seafood, such as shrimp, squid, mussels, and clams

2 tbsp chopped fresh oregano, plus extra to garnish

½ cup freshly grated romano or Parmesan cheese

salt and pepper

1 Heat the oil with half of the butter in a deep pan over medium heat until the butter has melted. Add the garlic and cook, stirring, for 1 minute.

2 Reduce the heat, add the rice, and mix to coat in oil and butter. Cook, stirring constantly, for 2–3 minutes, or until the grains are translucent.

3 Gradually add the hot stock, a ladleful at a time. Stir constantly and add more liquid as the rice absorbs each addition. Increase the heat to medium so that the liquid bubbles. Cook for 20 minutes, or until all the liquid is absorbed and the rice is creamy.

4 About 5 minutes before the rice is ready, add the seafood and oregano to the pan and mix well.

5 Remove the pan from the heat and season to taste. Add the remaining butter and mix well, then stir in the grated cheese until it melts. Spoon onto warmed plates and serve at once, garnished with extra oregano.

Fish & Rice with Dark Rum

INGREDIENTS

serves 4

1 lb/450 g firm white fish fillets (such as cod or angler fish), skinned and cut into 1-inch/2.5-cm cubes

2 tsp ground cumin

2 tsp dried oregano

2 tbsp lime juice

⅔ cup dark rum

1 tbsp molasses sugar

3 garlic cloves, chopped finely

1 large onion, chopped

1 each medium red bell pepper, green bell pepper, and yellow bell pepper, seeded and sliced into rings

5 cups fish stock

1¾ cups long-grain rice

salt and pepper

fresh oregano leaves, to garnish

lime wedges, to garnish

1 Place the cubes of fish in a bowl and add the cumin, oregano, lime juice, rum, and sugar. Season to taste with salt and pepper. Mix thoroughly, cover with plastic wrap, and set aside to chill for 2 hours.

2 Meanwhile, place the garlic, onion, and bell peppers in a large pan. Pour in the stock and stir in the rice. Bring to a boil, lower the heat, cover, and simmer for 15 minutes.

3 Gently stir in the fish and the marinade juices. Bring back to a boil and simmer, uncovered, stirring occasionally but taking care not to break up the fish, for about 10 minutes, until the fish is cooked and the rice is tender.

4 Season with salt and pepper and transfer to a warmed serving plate. Garnish with fresh oregano and lime wedges and serve.

Spicy Tuna with Fennel & Onion

INGREDIENTS

serves **4**

**4 tuna steaks, about 5 oz/
140 g each**

**2 fennel bulbs, thickly sliced
lengthwise**

2 red onions, sliced

2 tbsp extra virgin olive oil

MARINADE

½ cup extra virgin olive oil

**4 garlic cloves, finely
chopped**

**4 fresh red chiles, seeded
and finely chopped**

**juice and finely grated rind
of 2 lemons**

**4 tbsp finely chopped fresh
flat-leaf parsley**

salt and pepper

1 Whisk all the marinade ingredients together in a small bowl. Put the tuna steaks in a large, shallow dish and spoon over 4 tablespoons of the marinade, turning until well coated. Cover and let marinate in the refrigerator for 30 minutes. Set aside the remaining marinade.

2 Heat a stovetop ridged grill pan over high heat. Put the fennel and onions in a separate bowl, add the oil, and toss well to coat. Add to the grill pan and cook for 5 minutes on each side, until just beginning to color. Transfer to 4 warmed serving plates, drizzle with the reserved marinade, and keep warm.

3 Add the tuna steaks to the grill pan and cook, turning once, for 4–5 minutes, until firm to the touch but still moist inside. Transfer the tuna to the serving plates and serve at once.

Swordfish with Tomatoes & Olives

INGREDIENTS

serves 4

2 tbsp olive oil

1 onion, finely chopped

1 celery stalk, finely chopped

4 oz/115 g green olives, pitted

1 lb/450 g tomatoes, chopped

3 tbsp bottled capers, drained

salt and pepper

4 swordfish steaks, about 5 oz/140 g each

fresh flat-leaf parsley sprigs, to garnish

1 Heat the oil in a large, heavy-bottom pan. Add the onion and celery and cook over low heat, stirring occasionally, for 5 minutes, or until softened.

2 Meanwhile, roughly chop half the olives. Stir the chopped and whole olives into the pan with the tomatoes and capers and season to taste with salt and pepper.

3 Bring to a boil, then reduce the heat, cover, and simmer gently, stirring occasionally, for 15 minutes.

4 Add the swordfish steaks to the pan and return to a boil. Cover and simmer, turning the fish once, for 20 minutes, or until the fish is cooked and the flesh flakes easily. Transfer the fish to serving plates and spoon the sauce over them. Garnish with parsley and serve immediately.

Monkfish Packages

INGREDIENTS

4 tsp olive oil

2 zucchini, sliced

1 large red bell pepper, peeled, seeded, and cut into strips

2 monkfish fillets, about 4½ oz/125 g each, skin and membrane removed

6 smoked lean bacon slices

salt and pepper

TO SERVE

freshly cooked pasta

slices of olive bread

serves ❹

1 Preheat the oven to 375°F/190°C. Cut 4 large pieces of foil, about 9-inches/23-cm square. Brush lightly with a little of the oil, then divide the zucchini and bell pepper among them.

2 Rinse the fish fillets under cold running water and pat dry with paper towels. Cut them in half, then put 1 piece on top of each pile of zucchini and bell pepper. Cut the bacon slices in half and lay 3 pieces across each piece of fish. Season to taste with salt and pepper, drizzle over the remaining oil, and close up the packages. Seal tightly, transfer to an ovenproof dish, and bake in the preheated oven for 25 minutes.

3 Remove from the oven, open each foil package slightly, and serve with pasta and slices of olive bread.

Roasted Monkfish

INGREDIENTS

serves 4

1 lb 8 oz/675 g monkfish tail, skinned

4–5 large garlic cloves, peeled

3 tbsp olive oil

1 onion, cut into wedges

1 eggplant, about 10½ oz/ 300 g, cut into chunks

1 red bell pepper, seeded, cut into wedges

1 yellow bell pepper, seeded, cut into wedges

1 large zucchini, about 8 oz/ 225 g, cut into wedges

salt and pepper

1 tbsp shredded fresh basil, to garnish

1 Preheat the oven to 400°F/200°C. Remove the central bone from the fish if not already removed and make small slits down each fillet. Cut 2 of the garlic cloves into thin slivers and insert into the fish. Place the fish on a sheet of parchment paper, season with salt and pepper to taste, and drizzle over 1 tablespoon of the oil. Bring the top edges together. Form into a pleat and fold over, then fold the ends underneath, completely encasing the fish. Set aside.

2 Put the remaining garlic cloves and all the vegetables into a roasting pan and drizzle with the remaining oil, turning the vegetables so that they are well coated in the oil.

3 Roast in the preheated oven for 20 minutes, turning occasionally. Put the fish package on top of the vegetables and cook for an additional 15–20 minutes, or until the vegetables are tender and the fish is cooked.

4 Remove from the oven and open up the package. Cut the monkfish into thick slices. Arrange the vegetables on warmed serving plates, top with the fish slices, and sprinkle with the basil. Serve at once.

Roasted Seafood

INGREDIENTS

serves 4

1 lb 5 oz/600 g new potatoes

3 red onions, cut into wedges

2 zucchini, cut into chunks

8 garlic cloves, peeled but left whole

2 lemons, cut into wedges

4 fresh rosemary sprigs

4 tbsp olive oil

12 oz/350 g unshelled raw shrimp

2 small raw squid, cut into rings

4 tomatoes, quartered

1 Preheat the oven to 400°F/200°C. Scrub the potatoes to remove any dirt. Cut any large potatoes in half and parboil them in a pan of boiling water for 10–15 minutes.

2 Place the potatoes in a large roasting pan together with the onions, zucchini, garlic, lemons, and rosemary sprigs.

3 Pour over the oil and toss to coat all the vegetables in it. Roast in the oven for 30 minutes, turning occasionally, until the potatoes are tender.

4 Once the potatoes are tender, add the shrimp, squid, and tomatoes, tossing to coat them in the oil, and roast for 10 minutes. All the vegetables should be cooked through and slightly charred for full flavor. Transfer the roasted seafood and vegetables to warmed serving plates and serve hot.

Spicy Scallops with Lime & Chile

INGREDIENTS

16 large scallops

1 tbsp butter

1 tbsp vegetable oil

1 tsp minced garlic

1 tsp fresh ginger, grated

bunch of scallions, sliced thinly

finely grated peel of 1 lime

1 small fresh red chile, seeded and very finely chopped

3 tbsp lime juice

lime wedges, to serve

cooked rice, to serve

serves ❹

1 Trim the scallops, then wash, and pat dry. Separate the corals from the white parts, then slice each white part in half horizontally, making 2 circles.

2 Heat the butter and vegetable oil in a wok or skillet. Add the garlic and ginger and stir-fry for 1 minute without browning. Add the scallions and stir-fry for 1 minute.

3 Add the scallops and stir-fry over high heat for 4–5 minutes. Stir in the lime peel, chile, and lime juice and cook for 1 minute more.

4 Serve the scallops hot, with the juices spooned over them, accompanied by lime wedges and cooked rice.

Fresh Baked Sardines

INGREDIENTS

2 tbsp olive oil

2 large onions, sliced into rings

3 garlic cloves, chopped

2 large zucchini, cut into sticks

3 tbsp fresh thyme, stalks removed

8 large sardine fillets

1 cup grated Parmesan cheese

4 eggs, beaten

⅔ cup milk

salt and pepper

serves ❹

1 Preheat the oven to 350°F/180°C. Heat 1 tablespoon of the olive oil in a skillet. Add the onion rings and chopped garlic and fry over a low heat, stirring occasionally, for 2–3 minutes.

2 Add the zucchini to the skillet and cook, stirring occasionally, for about 5 minutes or until golden. Stir in 2 tablespoons of the thyme.

3 Place half the onions and zucchini in the bottom of a large ovenproof dish. Top with the sardine fillets and half the grated Parmesan cheese.

4 Place the remaining onions and zucchini on top and sprinkle with the remaining thyme.

5 Combine the eggs and milk in a bowl and season to taste with salt and pepper. Pour the mixture over the vegetables and sardines in the dish. Sprinkle the remaining Parmesan cheese over the top.

6 Bake for 20–25 minutes or until golden and set. Serve immediately.

4 Vegetables

Thick hearty vegetable soups, such as minestrone or French onion soup, provide a satisfying meal-in-a-bowl, while the earthy mellow flavors of beans and grains combine with fresh vegetables to make nutritious and deeply satisfying stews. There are also recipes in this chapter for risottos and gratins, Asian-style egg-fried rice and an irresistible vegetable pie. All can be prepared in only one pot, dish, or pan, leaving you with minimum cleaning up.

Chunky Vegetable Soup

INGREDIENTS

serves 6

2 carrots, sliced

1 onion, diced

1 garlic clove, crushed

12 oz/350 g new potatoes, diced

2 celery stalks, sliced

4 oz/115 g button mushrooms, quartered

14 oz/400 g canned chopped tomatoes, with their juice

2½ cups vegetable stock

1 bay leaf

1 tsp dried mixed herbs or 1 tbsp chopped fresh mixed herbs

½ cup corn kernels, frozen or canned, drained

2 oz/55 g green cabbage, shredded

pepper

crusty whole wheat or white bread rolls, to serve

1 Put the carrots, onion, garlic, potatoes, celery, mushrooms, tomatoes, and stock into a large pan. Stir in the bay leaf and herbs. Bring to a boil, then reduce the heat, cover, and let simmer for 25 minutes.

2 Add the corn and cabbage and return to a boil. Reduce the heat, cover, and let simmer for 5 minutes, or until the vegetables are tender. Remove and discard the bay leaf and season to taste with pepper.

3 Ladle into warmed bowls and serve at once with crusty bread rolls.

Minestrone

INGREDIENTS

serves ❹

2 tbsp olive oil

2 garlic cloves, chopped

2 red onions, chopped

2¾ oz/75 g prosciutto, sliced

**1 red bell pepper, seeded
and chopped**

**1 orange bell pepper, seeded
and chopped**

**14 oz/400 g canned chopped
tomatoes**

4 cups vegetable stock

**1 celery stalk, trimmed and
sliced**

**14 oz/400 g canned cranberry
beans, drained**

**3½ oz/100 g green leafy
cabbage, shredded**

**2¾ oz/75 g frozen peas,
thawed**

**1 tbsp chopped fresh
parsley**

salt and pepper

2¾ oz/75 g dried vermicelli

**freshly grated Parmesan
cheese, to garnish**

fresh crusty bread, to serve

1 Heat the oil in a large pan. Add the garlic, onions, and prosciutto and cook over medium heat, stirring, for 3 minutes, until slightly softened. Add the red and orange bell peppers and the chopped tomatoes and cook for another 2 minutes, stirring. Stir in the stock, then add the celery, beans, cabbage, peas, and parsley. Season with salt and pepper. Bring to a boil, then lower the heat and simmer for 30 minutes.

2 Add the vermicelli to the pan. Cook for another 10–12 minutes, or according to the instructions on the package. Remove from the heat and ladle into serving bowls. Garnish with freshly grated Parmesan and serve with fresh crusty bread.

French Onion Soup

INGREDIENTS

1 lb 8 oz/675 g onions

3 tbsp olive oil

**4 garlic cloves, 3 chopped
and 1 peeled but kept whole**

1 tsp sugar

2 tsp chopped fresh thyme

2 tbsp all-purpose flour

½ cup dry white wine

8 cups vegetable stock

6 slices of French bread

3 cups grated Swiss cheese

**fresh thyme sprigs,
to garnish**

serves ❻

1 Thinly slice the onions. Heat the olive oil in a large, heavy-bottom pan, then add the onions and cook, stirring occasionally, for 10 minutes, until they are just beginning to brown. Stir in the chopped garlic, sugar, and thyme, then reduce the heat and cook, stirring occasionally, for 30 minutes, or until the onions are golden brown.

2 Sprinkle in the flour and cook, stirring, for 1–2 minutes. Stir in the wine. Gradually stir in the stock and bring to a boil, skimming off any foam that rises to the surface, then reduce the heat and simmer for 45 minutes. Meanwhile, toast the bread on both sides under a preheated medium broiler. Rub the toast with the whole garlic clove.

3 Ladle the soup into 6 flameproof bowls set on a cookie sheet. Float a piece of toast in each bowl and divide the grated cheese among them. Place under a preheated medium–hot broiler for 2–3 minutes, or until the cheese has just melted. Garnish with thyme and serve.

Borscht

INGREDIENTS

1 onion

4 tbsp butter

12 oz/350 g raw beets, cut into thin sticks, and 1 raw beet, grated

1 carrot, cut into thin sticks

3 celery stalks, thinly sliced

2 tomatoes, peeled, seeded, and chopped

6¼ cups vegetable stock

1 tbsp white wine vinegar

1 tbsp sugar

2 tbsp snipped fresh dill

4 oz/115 g white cabbage, shredded

salt and pepper

⅔ cup sour cream, to garnish

crusty bread, to serve

serves ❻

1 Slice the onion into rings. Melt the butter in a large, heavy-bottom pan. Add the onion and cook over low heat, stirring occasionally, for 3–5 minutes, or until softened. Add the sticks of beet, carrot, celery, and chopped tomatoes and cook, stirring frequently, for 4–5 minutes.

2 Add the stock, vinegar, sugar, and 1 tablespoon of the snipped dill into the pan. Season to taste with salt and pepper. Bring to a boil, reduce the heat, and simmer for 35–40 minutes, or until the vegetables are tender.

3 Stir in the cabbage, cover, and simmer for 10 minutes, then stir in the grated beet, with any juices, and cook for an additional 10 minutes. Ladle the borscht into warmed bowls. Garnish with sour cream and another tablespoon of snipped dill and serve with crusty bread.

Vegetable Soup with Pesto

INGREDIENTS

serves **4**

4 cups fresh cold water

bouquet garni of 1 fresh parsley sprig, 1 fresh thyme sprig, and 1 bay leaf, tied together with clean string

2 celery stalks, chopped

3 baby leeks, chopped

4 baby carrots, chopped

5½ oz/150 g new potatoes, scrubbed and cut into bite-size chunks

4 tbsp shelled fava beans or peas

6 oz/175 g canned cannellini or flageolet beans, drained and rinsed

3 heads bok choy

scant 3¼ cups arugula

2 tbsp prepared pesto

pepper

1 Put the water and bouquet garni into a large pan and add the celery, leeks, carrots, and potatoes. Bring to a boil, then reduce the heat and let simmer for 10 minutes.

2 Stir in the fava beans or peas and canned beans and let simmer for an additional 10 minutes. Stir in the bok choy, arugula, and pepper to taste and let simmer for an additional 2–3 minutes. Remove and discard the bouquet garni.

3 Stir most of the pesto into the soup, then ladle into warmed bowls. Top with the remaining pesto and serve at once.

Spring Stew

INGREDIENTS

serves **4**

2 tbsp olive oil

4–8 pearl onions, halved

2 celery stalks, sliced

8 oz/225 g baby carrots, scrubbed and halved if large

10½ oz/300 g new potatoes, scrubbed and halved, or cut into quarters if large

3¾–5 cups vegetable stock

heaping 2¾ cups canned cannellini beans, drained and rinsed

1½–2 tbsp light soy sauce

3 oz/85 g baby corn

1 cup fresh fava beans

½–1 savoy cabbage

1½ tbsp cornstarch

2 tbsp cold water

salt and pepper

½–¾ cup grated **Parmesan** or sharp cheddar cheese, grated, to serve

1 Heat the oil in a large, heavy-bottom pan with a tight-fitting lid, and cook the onions, celery, carrots, and potatoes, stirring frequently, for 5 minutes, or until softened. Add the stock, drained beans, and soy sauce, then bring to a boil. Reduce the heat, then cover and simmer for 12 minutes.

2 Add the baby corn and fava beans and season to taste with salt and pepper. Simmer for an additional 3 minutes.

3 Meanwhile, discard the outer leaves and hard central core from the cabbage and shred the leaves. Add to the pan and simmer for an additional 3–5 minutes, or until all the vegetables are tender.

4 Blend the cornstarch with the water, then stir into the pan and cook, stirring, for 4–6 minutes, or until the liquid has thickened. Serve the cheese separately, for stirring into the stew.

Tuscan Bean Stew

INGREDIENTS

serves 4

1 large fennel bulb

2 tbsp olive oil

1 red onion, cut into small wedges

2–4 garlic cloves, sliced

1 small eggplant, about 8 oz/ 225 g, cut into chunks

2 tbsp tomato paste

scant 2–2½ cups vegetable stock

1 lb/450 g ripe tomatoes

a few sprigs of fresh oregano

14 oz/400 g canned cranberry beans

14 oz/400 g canned flageolets

1 yellow bell pepper, seeded and cut into small strips

1 zucchini, sliced into semicircles

⅓ cup pitted black olives

25 g/1 oz Parmesan cheese, freshly shaved

salt and pepper

crusty bread, to serve

1 Trim the fennel and reserve any feathery fronds, then cut the bulb into small strips. Heat the oil in a large, heavy-bottom pan with a tight-fitting lid, and cook the onion, garlic, and fennel strips, stirring frequently, for 5–8 minutes, or until softened.

2 Add the eggplant and cook, stirring frequently, for 5 minutes. Blend the tomato paste with a little of the stock in a pitcher and pour over the fennel mixture, then add the remaining stock, and the tomatoes, and oregano. Bring to a boil, then reduce the heat and simmer, covered, for 15 minutes, or until the tomatoes have begun to collapse.

3 Drain and rinse the beans, then drain again. Add them to the pan with the yellow bell pepper, zucchini, and olives. Simmer for an additional 15 minutes, or until the vegetables are tender. Taste and adjust the seasoning. Scatter with the Parmesan shavings and serve garnished with the reserved fennel fronds, accompanied by crusty bread.

Chile Bean Stew

INGREDIENTS

serves 4 to 6

2 tbsp olive oil

1 onion, chopped

2–4 garlic cloves, chopped

2 fresh red chiles, seeded and sliced

1⅔ cups canned kidney beans, drained and rinsed

1⅔ cups canned cannellini beans, drained and rinsed

1⅔ cups canned chickpeas, drained and rinsed

1 tbsp tomato paste

3¾ cups stock

1 red bell pepper, seeded and chopped

4 tomatoes, coarsely chopped

1½ cups fresh fava beans

1 tbsp chopped fresh cilantro

pepper

sour cream, to serve

chopped cilantro and paprika, to garnish

1 Heat the oil in a large, heavy-bottom pan with a tight-fitting lid, and cook the onion, garlic, and chiles, stirring frequently, for 5 minutes, or until softened. Add the kidney and cannellini beans and the chickpeas. Blend the tomato paste with a little of the stock in a pitcher and pour over the bean mixture, then add the remaining stock. Bring to a boil, then reduce the heat and simmer for 10–15 minutes.

2 Add the red bell pepper, tomatoes, fava beans, and pepper to taste and simmer for 15–20 minutes, or until all the vegetables are tender. Stir in the chopped cilantro.

3 Serve the stew topped with spoonfuls of sour cream and garnished with chopped cilantro and a pinch of paprika.

Potato & Lemon Casserole

INGREDIENTS

serves **4**

scant ½ cup olive oil

2 red onions, cut into
8 wedges

3 garlic cloves, crushed

2 tsp ground cumin

2 tsp ground coriander

pinch of cayenne pepper

1 carrot, thickly sliced

2 small turnips, quartered

1 zucchini, sliced

1 lb 2 oz/500 g potatoes,
thickly sliced

juice and grated rind of
2 large lemons

1¼ cups vegetable stock

salt and pepper

2 tbsp chopped fresh
cilantro, to garnish

1 Heat the olive oil in a flameproof casserole. Add the onions and sauté over medium heat, stirring frequently, for 3 minutes.

2 Add the garlic and cook for 30 seconds. Stir in the ground cumin, ground coriander, and cayenne and cook, stirring constantly, for 1 minute.

3 Add the carrot, turnips, zucchini, and potatoes and stir to coat in the oil.

4 Add the lemon juice and rind and the vegetable stock. Season to taste with salt and pepper. Cover and cook over medium heat, stirring occasionally, for 20–30 minutes, until tender.

5 Remove the lid, sprinkle in the chopped fresh cilantro, and stir well. Serve immediately.

Lentil & Rice Casserole

INGREDIENTS

1 cup red lentils

heaping ¼ cup long-grain rice

5 cups vegetable stock

1 leek, cut into chunks

3 garlic cloves, crushed

14 oz/400 g canned chopped tomatoes, with their juice

1 tsp ground cumin

1 tsp chili powder

1 tsp garam masala

1 red bell pepper, seeded and sliced

3½ oz/100 g small broccoli florets

8 baby corn, halved lengthwise

2 oz/55 g green beans, halved

1 tbsp shredded fresh basil

salt and pepper

fresh basil sprigs, to garnish

serves ❹

1 Place the lentils, rice, and vegetable stock in a large flameproof casserole and cook over low heat, stirring occasionally, for 20 minutes.

2 Add the leek, garlic, tomatoes and their juice, ground cumin, chili powder, garam masala, sliced bell pepper, broccoli, baby corn, and green beans to the casserole.

3 Bring the mixture to a boil, reduce the heat, cover, and simmer for an additional 10–15 minutes, or until all the vegetables are tender.

4 Add the shredded basil and season with salt and pepper to taste.

5 Garnish with fresh basil sprigs and serve immediately.

Asian-Style Rice Pilau

INGREDIENTS

serves 4

1 tbsp vegetable oil

1 bunch scallions, white and green parts, chopped

1 garlic clove, crushed

1 tsp fresh ginger, grated

1 orange bell pepper, seeded and diced

1½ cups rice grains

2½ cups water

1 orange

⅔ cup chopped pitted dates

2 tsp sesame oil

1 cup roasted cashew nuts

2 tbsp pumpkin seeds

salt and pepper

Asian salad vegetables, to serve

1 Heat the oil in a pan. Add the scallions, garlic, ginger, and bell pepper and cook over medium heat, stirring frequently, for 2–3 minutes, until just softened, but not browned. Add the rice and pour in the water.

2 Using a vegetable peeler, pare the rind from the orange and add the rind to the pan. Squeeze the juice from the orange into the pan. Season to taste with salt and pepper.

3 Bring to a boil, reduce the heat, cover, and cook gently for 20 minutes, until all the liquid has been absorbed. Remove the pan from the heat, stir in the dates and sesame oil, and set aside to stand for 10 minutes.

4 Remove and discard the orange rind and stir in the cashew nuts. Pile into a warmed serving dish, sprinkle with pumpkin seeds, and serve immediately with Asian salad vegetables.

Risotto with Artichoke Hearts

INGREDIENTS

8 oz/225 g canned artichoke hearts

1 tbsp olive oil

3 tbsp butter

1 small onion, finely chopped

scant 1½ cups risotto rice

5 cups boiling vegetable stock

¾ cup freshly grated Parmesan or Grana Padano cheese

salt and pepper

fresh flat-leaf parsley sprigs, to garnish

serves ❹

1 Drain the artichoke hearts, reserving the liquid, and cut them into quarters.

2 Heat the oil with 2 tablespoons of the butter in a deep pan over medium heat until the butter has melted. Stir in the onion and cook gently, stirring occasionally, for 5 minutes, or until soft and starting to turn golden. Do not brown.

3 Add the rice and mix to coat in oil and butter. Cook, stirring constantly, for 2–3 minutes, or until the grains are translucent.

4 Gradually add the artichoke liquid and the hot stock, a ladle at a time. Stir constantly and add more liquid as the rice absorbs each addition. Increase the heat to medium so that the liquid bubbles. Cook for 15 minutes, then add the artichoke hearts. Cook for an additional 5 minutes, or until all the liquid is absorbed and the rice is creamy. Season to taste.

5 Remove the risotto from the heat and add the remaining butter. Mix well, then stir in the Parmesan until it melts. Season, if necessary. Spoon the risotto into warmed bowls, garnish with parsley sprigs, and serve at once.

Egg-Fried Rice with Vegetables

INGREDIENTS

serves ❻ to ❽

2 tbsp vegetable or peanut oil

2 garlic cloves, finely chopped

2 fresh red chiles, seeded and chopped

2 cups button mushrooms, sliced

2 oz/55 g snow peas, halved

2 oz/55 g baby corn, halved

3 tbsp Thai soy sauce

1 tbsp light brown sugar

a few Thai basil leaves

3 cups rice, cooked and cooled

2 eggs, beaten

CRISPY ONION TOPPING (OPTIONAL)

2 tbsp vegetable or peanut oil

2 onions, sliced

1 Heat the oil in a wok or large skillet and sauté the garlic and chiles for 2–3 minutes.

2 Add the mushrooms, snow peas, and corn, and stir-fry for 2–3 minutes before adding the soy sauce, sugar, and basil. Stir in the rice.

3 Push the mixture to one side of the wok and add the eggs to the bottom. Stir until lightly set before combining into the rice mixture.

4 If you want to make the crispy onion topping, heat the oil in another skillet and sauté the onions until crispy and brown. Serve the rice topped with the onions.

Vegetable Toad-in-the-Hole

INGREDIENTS

serves ❹

¾ cup all-purpose flour

2 eggs, beaten

¾ cup milk

2 tbsp whole grain mustard

2 tbsp vegetable oil

FILLING

2 tbsp butter

2 garlic cloves, crushed

1 onion, cut into eight

18 baby carrots, halved lengthwise

⅔ cup green beans

¼ cup canned corn, drained

2 tomatoes, seeded and cut into chunks

1 tsp whole grain mustard

1 tbsp chopped mixed herbs

salt and pepper

1 Preheat the oven to 400°F/200°C. To make the batter, sift the flour and a pinch of salt into a bowl. Beat in the eggs and milk to make a batter. Stir in the mustard and let stand.

2 Pour the oil into a shallow ovenproof dish and heat in the preheated oven for 10 minutes.

3 To make the filling, melt the butter in a skillet and sauté the garlic and onion, stirring constantly, for 2 minutes. Cook the carrots and beans in a pan of boiling water for 7 minutes, or until tender. Drain well.

4 Add the corn and tomatoes to the skillet with the mustard and chopped mixed herbs. Season well and add the carrots and beans.

5 Remove the heated dish from the oven and pour in the batter. Spoon the vegetables into the center, return to the oven, and cook for 30–35 minutes, until the batter has risen and set. Serve immediately.

Eggplant Gratin

INGREDIENTS

4 tbsp olive oil

2 onions, finely chopped

2 garlic cloves, very finely chopped

2 eggplants, thickly sliced

3 tbsp fresh flat-leaf parsley, chopped

½ tsp dried thyme

14 oz/400 g canned chopped tomatoes

1½ cups coarsely grated mozzarella

6 tbsp freshly grated Parmesan

salt and pepper

serves ❷

1 Preheat the oven to 400°F/200°C. Heat the oil in a flameproof casserole over medium heat. Add the onion and cook for 5 minutes, or until soft. Add the garlic and cook for a few seconds, or until just beginning to color. Using a slotted spoon, transfer the onion mixture to a plate.

2 Cook the eggplant slices in batches in the same flameproof casserole until they are just lightly browned. Transfer to another plate.

3 Arrange a layer of eggplant slices in the bottom of the casserole dish or a shallow ovenproof dish. Sprinkle with a little of the parsley and thyme, and season to taste.

4 Add a layer of onion, tomatoes, mozzarella, and a sprinkling of parsley, thyme, and seasoning over each layer.

5 Continue layering, finishing with a layer of eggplant slices. Sprinkle with the Parmesan. Bake, uncovered, for 20–30 minutes, or until the top is golden and the eggplants are tender. Serve hot.

Roast Summer Vegetables

INGREDIENTS

2 tbsp olive oil

1 fennel bulb, cut into wedges

2 red onions, cut into wedges

2 beefsteak tomatoes, cut into wedges

1 eggplant, thickly sliced

2 zucchini, thickly sliced

1 yellow bell pepper, seeded and cut into chunks

1 red bell pepper, seeded and cut into chunks

1 orange bell pepper, seeded and cut into chunks

4 garlic cloves

4 fresh rosemary sprigs

ground black pepper

crusty bread, to serve (optional)

serves ❹

1 Preheat the oven to 400°F/200°C. Prepare the vegetables. Brush an ovenproof dish with a little oil. Arrange the fennel, onions, tomatoes, eggplant, zucchini, and bell peppers in the dish and tuck the garlic cloves and rosemary sprigs among them. Drizzle with the remaining oil and season to taste with pepper.

2 Roast the vegetables in the preheated oven for 10 minutes.

3 Turn the vegetables over, return the dish to the oven, and roast for an additional 10–15 minutes, or until the vegetables are tender and beginning to turn golden brown.

4 Serve the vegetables straight from the dish or transfer to a warm serving platter. Serve immediately, with crusty bread, if you like, to soak up the juices.

5 Desserts

Cooked fruit desserts lend themselves admirably to one-pot cooking—the dish can be brought straight from the stove to the table, and there are no sticky bowls or whisks to clean up. The recipes include comforting favorites, such as crumbles, crisps, and cobblers, as well as a stunning blueberry sweet batter pudding. You'll also find recipes for a glamorous chocolate fondue, an easy-to-make one-roll pie, and a bread-and-butter dessert to die for.

Apple & Blackberry Crumble

INGREDIENTS

2 lb/900 g tart cooking apples, peeled and sliced

10½ oz/300 g blackberries, fresh or frozen

¼ cup brown sugar

1 tsp ground cinnamon

light or heavy cream, to serve

CRUMBLE TOPPING

⅔ cup self-rising flour

⅔ cup whole wheat all-purpose flour

½ cup butter

¼ cup raw brown sugar

serves **4**

1 Preheat the oven to 400°F/200°C. Peel and core the apples and cut into chunks. Place in a bowl with the blackberries, sugar, and cinnamon and mix together, then transfer to an ovenproof baking dish.

2 To make the crumble topping, sift the self-rising flour into a bowl and stir in the whole wheat flour. Add the butter and rub it in with your fingertips until the mixture resembles fine breadcrumbs. Stir in the sugar.

3 Spread the crumble over the apples and bake in the preheated oven for 40–45 minutes, or until the apples are soft and the crumble is golden brown and crisp. Serve with cream.

Rhubarb Crumble

INGREDIENTS

2 lb/900 g rhubarb

½ cup superfine sugar

grated rind and juice of 1 orange

cream, yogurt, or custard, to serve

CRUMBLE TOPPING

heaping 1½ cups all-purpose or whole wheat flour

½ cup butter, diced and chilled

½ cup light brown sugar

1 tsp ground ginger

serves ❻

1 Preheat the oven to 375°F/190°C.

2 Cut the rhubarb into 1-inch/2.5-cm lengths and put in an ovenproof dish with the superfine sugar and orange rind and juice.

3 To make the crumble topping, sift the flour into a bowl. Rub in the butter with your fingertips until the mixture resembles fine breadcrumbs. Stir in the brown sugar and ginger. Spread evenly over the fruit and press down lightly with a fork.

4 Bake in the center of the preheated oven for 25–30 minutes, until the crumble is golden brown.

5 Serve warm with cream.

Sherried Nectarine Crumble

INGREDIENTS

serves ❹

6 nectarines

2 tbsp raw sugar

2 tbsp sweet sherry

light or heavy cream, to serve

CRUMBLE TOPPING

1¼ cups all-purpose flour

¼ cup raw sugar, plus extra for sprinkling

½ cup unsalted butter, melted

1 Preheat the oven to 400°F/200°C. Using a sharp knife, halve the nectarines, remove and discard the pits, then cut the flesh into fairly thick slices. Put the nectarine slices into an ovenproof saucepan, sprinkle over the sugar and sweet sherry, then cook in the preheated oven for 5–10 minutes, until heated through.

2 To make the crumble topping, put the flour and sugar in a large bowl, then quickly mix in the melted butter until crumbly. Carefully arrange the crumble over the nectarines in an even layer—keep your touch light or the crumble will sink into the filling and become mushy. Sprinkle a little more sugar over the top, then transfer to the preheated oven and bake for 25–30 minutes, or until the crumble topping is golden brown.

3 Remove from the oven and serve with generous spoonfuls of cream.

Peach & Orange Crumble

INGREDIENTS

6 peaches

2 tbsp raw sugar

2 tbsp orange juice

**light or heavy cream,
to serve**

CRUMBLE TOPPING

¾ cup self-rising flour

½ cup unsalted butter, diced

5 tbsp raw brown sugar

**3 tbsp finely chopped
hazelnuts**

serves ❹

1 Preheat the oven to 400°F/200°C. Using a sharp knife, halve the peaches, remove and discard the pits, then cut the flesh into fairly thick slices. Put the peach slices into an ovenproof saucepan, sprinkle over the sugar and orange juice, then cook in the preheated oven for 5–10 minutes, until heated through.

2 To make the crumble topping, put the flour in a large bowl, then rub in the butter with your fingertips, until the mixture resembles fine breadcrumbs. Stir in 4 tablespoons of the sugar and the hazelnuts. Carefully arrange the crumble over the peaches in an even layer—keep your touch light or the crumble will sink into the filling and go mushy. Scatter the remaining sugar over the top, then transfer to the preheated oven and bake for 25–30 minutes, or until the crumble topping is golden brown.

3 Remove from the oven and serve with cream.

Deep Chocolate Crumble

INGREDIENTS

serves **4**

2¼ oz/60 g unsweetened cocoa

1 cup water

⅔ cup superfine sugar

2 tbsp unsalted butter, diced

4 large cooking apples

CRUMBLE TOPPING

¾ cup self-rising flour

1 tbsp unsweetened cocoa

½ cup unsalted butter, diced

5 tbsp dark brown sugar

2 tbsp finely chopped pecans

1¾ oz/50 g semisweet chocolate, finely chopped

1 Preheat the oven to 350°F/180°C. To make the crumble topping, put the flour and cocoa in a large mixing bowl, then rub in the butter with your fingertips until the mixture resembles fine breadcrumbs. Stir in 4 tablespoons of the sugar and the chopped pecans, then stir in the chopped chocolate and set aside.

2 To make the filling, put the cocoa, water, and superfine sugar in a small saucepan and cook, stirring, over low heat for 3 minutes. Add the diced butter and return to a simmer, stirring constantly, then remove from the heat.

3 Peel and slice the apples, then spread them evenly in the bottom of an ovenproof saucepan (this has to be done quickly to prevent the apples from discoloring). Pour over half of the chocolate sauce, then sprinkle over the crumble topping. Scatter over the remaining sugar. Bake in the preheated oven for about 20–25 minutes, or until the crumble topping is cooked. Just before the end of the cooking time, return the remaining chocolate sauce to the stovetop and warm gently. Remove the crumble from the oven and serve with the warmed chocolate sauce.

Fruit Cobbler

INGREDIENTS

2 lb/900 g fresh or thawed frozen berries

½ cup superfine sugar

2 tbsp cornstarch

light or heavy cream, to serve

COBBLER TOPPING

1⅓ cups all-purpose flour

2 tsp baking powder

pinch of salt

4 tbsp unsalted butter, diced and chilled

2 tbsp superfine sugar

¾ cup buttermilk

1 tbsp raw sugar

serves 6

1 Preheat the oven to 400°F/200°C. Pick over the fruit, then mix with the superfine sugar and cornstarch and put in a 10-inch/25-cm shallow, ovenproof dish.

2 To make the cobbler topping, sift the flour, baking powder, and salt into a large bowl. Rub in the butter with your fingertips until the mixture resembles fine breadcrumbs, then stir in the superfine sugar. Pour in the buttermilk and mix to a soft dough.

3 Drop spoonfuls of the dough on top of the fruit roughly, so that it doesn't completely cover the fruit. Sprinkle with the raw sugar and bake in the preheated oven for 25–30 minutes, or until the crust is golden and the fruit is tender.

4 Remove from the oven and let stand for a few minutes before serving with cream.

Strawberry Cream Cobbler

INGREDIENTS

serves 4

1 lb 12 oz/800 g strawberries, hulled and halved

¼ cup superfine sugar

whipped heavy cream

COBBLER TOPPING

1½ cups self-rising flour, plus extra for dusting

pinch of salt

3 tbsp butter

2 tbsp superfine sugar

1 egg, beaten

2 tbsp golden raisins

2 tbsp raisins

5 tbsp milk, plus extra for glazing

1 Preheat the oven to 400°F/200°C. Arrange the strawberries evenly in the bottom of an ovenproof saucepan, then sprinkle over the sugar and cook in the preheated oven for 5–10 minutes, until heated through.

2 To make the cobbler topping, sift the flour and salt into a large mixing bowl. Rub in the butter with your fingertips until the mixture resembles fine breadcrumbs, then stir in the sugar. Add the beaten egg, then the golden raisins and raisins and mix lightly until incorporated. Stir in enough of the milk to make a smooth dough. Transfer to a clean, lightly floured board, knead lightly, then roll out to a thickness of about ½ inch/1 cm. Cut out circles using a 2-inch/5-cm cookie cutter. Arrange the dough circles over the strawberries, then brush the tops with a little milk.

3 Bake in the preheated oven for 25–30 minutes, or until the cobbler topping has risen and is lightly golden. Remove from the oven and serve with whipped heavy cream.

Bread & Butter Dessert

INGREDIENTS

6 tbsp butter, softened

6 slices of thick white bread

⅓ cup mixed fruit

2 tbsp candied peel

3 large eggs

1¼ cups milk

⅔ cup heavy cream

¼ cup superfine sugar

whole nutmeg, for grating

1 tbsp raw sugar

cream, to serve

serves 4 to 6

1 Preheat the oven to 350°F/180°C.

2 Use a little of the butter to grease an 8 x 10-inch/20 x 25-cm baking dish and butter the slices of bread. Cut the bread into quarters and arrange half overlapping in the dish.

3 Scatter half the fruit and peel over the bread, cover with the remaining bread slices, and add the remaining fruit and peel.

4 In a mixing pitcher, whisk the eggs well and mix in the milk, cream, and sugar. Pour this over the dessert and let stand for 15 minutes to allow the bread to soak up some of the egg mixture. Tuck in most of the fruit because you don't want it to burn in the oven. Grate the nutmeg over the top of the dessert, according to taste, and sprinkle over the raw sugar.

5 Place the dessert on a baking tray and bake at the top of the oven for 30–40 minutes, until just set and golden brown.

6 Remove from the oven and serve warm with a little cream.

Baked Rice Dessert

INGREDIENTS

1 tbsp melted unsalted butter

½ cup white rice

¼ cup superfine sugar

3½ cups whole milk

½ tsp vanilla extract

3 tbsp unsalted butter, chilled and cut into pieces

whole nutmeg, for grating

cream, jam, fresh fruit purée, stewed fruit, honey, or ice cream, for serving

serves ❹ to ❻

1 Preheat the oven to 300°F/150°C. Grease a 1-quart/1.2-liter baking dish (a gratin dish is good) with the melted butter, place the rice in the dish, and sprinkle with the sugar.

2 Heat the milk in a saucepan until almost boiling, then pour over the rice. Add the vanilla extract and stir well to dissolve the sugar.

3 Scatter the pieces of butter over the surface of the dessert.

4 Grate the nutmeg over the top, using as much as you like to give it a good covering.

5 Place the dish on a cookie sheet and bake in the center of the oven for 1½–2 hours, until the dessert is well browned on top, stirring the dessert after the first half hour of cooking to disperse the rice.

6 Serve hot topped with cream, jam, fresh fruit puree, stewed fruit, honey, or ice cream.

Blueberry Clafoutis

INGREDIENTS

2 tbsp butter, for greasing

½ cup superfine sugar

3 eggs

½ cup all-purpose flour

1 cup light cream

½ tsp ground cinnamon

1 lb/450 g blueberries

confectioners' sugar, to decorate

light or heavy cream, to serve

serves ❹

1 Preheat the oven to 350°F/180°C.

2 Put the butter in a bowl with the sugar and cream together until fluffy. Add the eggs and beat together well. Mix in the flour, then gradually stir in the cream followed by the cinnamon. Continue to stir until smooth.

3 Arrange the blueberries in the bottom of the prepared dish, then pour over the cream batter. Transfer to the preheated oven and bake for about 30 minutes, or until puffed and golden.

4 Remove from the oven, dust with confectioners' sugar, and serve with cream.

One-Roll Fruit Pie

INGREDIENTS

serves 8

PASTRY

6 tbsp butter, cut into small pieces, plus extra for greasing

1¼ cups all-purpose flour

1 tbsp water

1 egg, separated

sugar lumps, crushed, for sprinkling

light or heavy cream, to serve

FILLING

1 lb 5 oz/600 g prepared fruit

⅓ cup packed brown sugar

1 tbsp ground ginger

1 Grease a large cookie sheet with a little butter and set aside until required.

2 To make the pie dough, place the flour and butter in a mixing bowl and rub in the butter with your fingertips, until the mixture resembles fine breadcrumbs. Add the water and work the mixture together until a soft dough has formed. Form into a ball. Wrap the dough and let chill in the refrigerator for 30 minutes.

3 Preheat the oven to 400°F/200°C. Roll out the chilled dough to a circle about 14 inches/35 cm in diameter.

4 Transfer the dough circle to the center of the prepared cookie sheet. Lightly beat the egg yolk, then brush the dough with it.

5 To make the filling, mix the fruit with the brown sugar and ground ginger. Pile it into the center of the dough.

6 Turn in the edges of the dough circle all the way around. Lightly beat the egg white, then brush the surface of the dough with it, and sprinkle with the crushed sugar lumps.

7 Bake in the preheated oven for 35 minutes, or until golden brown. Serve warm with cream.

Chocolate Fondue

INGREDIENTS

serves 6

1 pineapple

1 mango

12 Cape gooseberries (if unavailable, use 12 small cubes of firm sponge cake instead)

9 oz/250 g fresh strawberries

9 oz/250 g seedless green grapes

FONDUE

9 oz/250 g semisweet chocolate, broken into pieces

5 fl oz/150 ml heavy cream

⅔ cup brandy

1 Using a sharp knife, peel and core the pineapple, then cut the flesh into cubes. Peel the mango and cut the flesh into cubes. Peel back the papery outer skin of the Cape gooseberries and twist at the top to make a handle. Arrange all the fruit on 6 serving plates and let chill in the refrigerator.

2 To make the fondue, place the chocolate and cream in a fondue pot. Heat gently, stirring constantly, until the chocolate has melted. Stir in the brandy until thoroughly blended and the chocolate mixture is smooth.

3 Place the fondue pot over the burner to keep warm. To serve, let each guest dip the fruit into the sauce, using fondue forks or bamboo skewers.

Index